TO SEE THE KING

BY

JANIS WALKER

AUTHOR OF

ALLELUIA! A GOSPEL DIARY

Books by Janis Walker

ALLELUIA! A GOSPEL DIARY

FIRST READING: A DIARY

HALLELUJAH! A PSALM RESPONSE DIARY

SECOND READING: A DIARY

A TRIP TO GRACE

SHEPHERDS

MYSTERY!

MYSTICS AND MASHED POTATOES

TO SEE THE KING

TO SEE THE KING

BY

JANIS WALKER

PALLIUM PRESS

Unless otherwise noted, Scripture quotations are from The Revised Standard Version, Old Testament section copyright 1952, New Testament section copyright 1946 & 1971, by Division of Christian Education of the National Council of Churches of Christ in the United States of America.

Scripture quotations marked NRSV are from New Revised Standard Version Bible, copyright 1989, Division of Christian Education of the National Council of Churches of Christ in the United States of America.

Scripture quotations marked KJV are from the The King James Version of the Bible.

Every effort has been made to insure accuracy of text and quotations, and any errors or omissions brought to our attention will be corrected in future editions.

FIRST PRINTING 2016

Pallium Press, P.O. Box 60910, Palo Alto, CA 94306-0910
We regret that Pallium Press cannot accept or return unsolicited manuscripts.

Check for new titles by Janis Walker at www.palliumpress.com

Pallium Press books are available at www.Amazon.com, www.BarnesandNoble.com, or at your favorite local independent bookstore.

Front cover photo: Christ the King window, Our Lady of the Pillar Catholic Church,
Half Moon Bay, California
Back cover photos: detail of a window at The Church of the Nativity,
Menlo Park, California,
and San Francisco skies, all by Terry Walker

cover design: Janis Walker

Copyright © 2016 by Janis Walker

All rights reserved. No part of this book may be reproduced, transmitted, stored in a retrieval system, or otherwise copied by any means whether electrical, mechanical, optical, or recording without the express written consent of Pallium Press, except for brief excerpts as part of reviews as permitted under the 1976 United States Copyright Act.

Printed in the United States of America.

ISBN 978-0-9826883-9-7

For

Christopher, my son

and

Peter, my godson

Acknowledgments

Thank you to Terry and Christopher and for all my family and friends who encourage me to continue to write.

I am especially grateful for Joy Dawson's teachings and ministry, and for the ministry of others who encouraged me to study God's names.

"Thine eyes shall see the king in his beauty … (Isaiah 33, 17a <u>The Holy Bible, King James Version</u>)."

A.M.D.G.

20 November 2016

The Feast of Christ the King

This study on the names of God began many years ago when my son Christopher was in nursery school. I kept a huge loose-leaf note book in which I wrote out the various names of God, the Scripture references, and occasional reflections.

As the years went by I graduated from seminary and served in various ministries. Recently, I decided to go back over this book, and add a few reflections.

When I began the work, I studied mainly the <u>New Oxford Annotated Bible</u>, which is an ecumenical study Bible based on <u>The Revised Standard Version</u>. Unless otherwise noted, the Scripture references are from the RSV translation.

N.B. The <u>New American Bible</u> numbers the verses in the psalms according to the Hebrew Psalter. Other translations are usually one verse behind because their numbering is according to the Greek and Latin Psalters.

"O God, who on the holy mount revealed to chosen witnesses your well-beloved Son, wonderfully transfigured, in raiment white and glistening: Mercifully grant that we, being delivered from the disquietude of this world, may by faith behold the King in his beauty; who with you, O Father, and you, O Holy Spirit, lives and reigns, one God, for ever and ever. Amen."
Collect for the Feast of the Transfiguration
<u>The Book of Common Prayer</u>, p. 243

ABBA

In the Old Testament, references to God as Father were rare. Jesus, however, called God the Father "Abba," the tender, trusting "Daddy." "Abba" is the Aramaic translation for "Papa" or "Daddy."

Once, in a supermarket, I saw a small child riding in the baby-seat of a shopping cart. The child kept looking up with delight at the father and saying, "Abba, Abba!"

"When we cry, 'Abba! Father!' it is the Spirit himself bearing witness with our spirit that we are children of God... (Romans 8, 15b-16)."

"But when the fullness of time had come, God sent his Son, born of a woman, born under the law, in order to redeem those who were under the law, so that we might receive adoption as children. And because you are children, God sent the Spirit of his Son into our hearts, crying, 'Abba! Father!' So you are no longer a slave but a child, and if a child then also an heir, through God (Galatians 4, 4-7)." (<u>New Revised Standard Version</u> (NRSV))

In the garden of Gethsemane, Jesus prayed, " 'Abba, Father!' he said, 'For you everything is possible; remove this cup from me; yet, let it be as you, not what I want, but what you want (Mark 14, 36 NRSV).' "

ADONAY (one of the Hebrew words for "Lord")

The first time the name "Lord" (the translation of "Adonay") is found is in Genesis 15, 2 in which Abraham addresses God as "O LORD GOD."

ADVOCATE

This comes from the Greek word "parakletos," which means intercessor, consoler, and comforter.

"... if an one does sin, we have an advocate with the Father, Jesus Christ the righteous, and he is the atoning sacrifice for our sins, and not for ours only but also for the sins of the whole world (1 John 2, 1b-2 NRSV)."

<u>Merriam Webster's Collegiate Dictionary, Eleventh Edition</u>, defines advocate as "one that pleads the cause of another; specifically:

one that pleads the cause of another before a tribunal or judicial court." Jesus is our advocate, as well as our judge (Acts 10, 42). The one who is to be our judge knows all about us and even intercedes for us.

ALMIGHTY

"When Abram was ninety-nine years old the LORD appeared to Abram, and said to him, 'I am God Almighty; walk before me, and be blameless. And I will make my covenant between me and you, and will multiply you exceedingly.' Then Abram fell on his face; and God said to him, 'Behold, my covenant is with you, and you shall be the father of a multitude of nations. No longer shall your name be Abram, but your name shall be Abraham; for I have made you the father of a multitude of nations (Genesis 17, 1-5).' "

The name "Almighty" traditionally used here is "El Shaddai," meaning "God, the One of the Mountains."

To Abraham's grandson, Jacob, whose new name was Israel, God said, "… 'I am God Almighty: be fruitful and multiply; a nation and a company of nations shall come from you and kings shall spring from you … (Genesis 35, 11).' "

"You who live in the shelter of the Most High, who abide in the shadow of the Almighty, will say to the LORD, 'My refuge and my fortress; my God, in whom I trust (Psalm 91, 1 NRSV).' "

Job! In that amazing book of Job, we find more references to God as the Almighty than in any other book of the Old Testament.

One of the references comes from Elihu, the only one of Job's friends who did not arouse God's anger. "Out of the north comes golden splendor; God is clothed with terrible majesty. The Almighty-- we cannot find him; he is great in power and justice, and abundant righteousness he will not violate (Job 37, 22-23)."

" 'I am the Alpha and the Omega,' says the Lord God, who is and who was and who is to come, the Almighty (Revelation 1, 8).' "

The following three verses are all part of the scene in heaven, recorded in the book of the Revelation.

" 'Holy, holy, holy, is the Lord God Almighty,
   who was and is and is to come(Revelation 4,8)!' "

"And I saw what appeared to be a sea of glass mingled with fire, and those who had conquered the beast and its image and the number of its name, standing beside the sea of glass with harps of God in their hands. And they sing the song of Moses, the servant of God, and the song of the Lamb, saying,

> 'Great and wonderful are thy deeds,
> O Lord God the Almighty!
> Just and true are thy ways,
> O King of the ages (Revelation 15, 1-3)!' "

"And I saw no temple in the city, for its Temple is the Lord God the Almighty and the Lamb. (Revelation 21, 2)."

"... I will be a Father to you,
and you shall be my sons and daughters,
says the Lord Almighty. (2 Corinthians 6, 18)."

The word "Almighty" in these New Testament passages is "pantokrator," which means God as absolute, omnipotent sovereign.

We are reminded of the glorious Hallelujah Chorus from Handel's "Messiah" ("And He shall reign for ever and ever!").

Now, and later in our study when we look at the kingship of God in greater detail, we can rejoice that this powerful Almighty One is our loving Father.

ALPHA AND OMEGA

"I am the Alpha and the Omega,
    the first and the last,
        the beginning and the end (Revelation 22, 13)."

"Alpha" is the first letter of the Greek alphabet and "Omega" is the last, "the finality."

" 'I am the Alpha and the Omega,' says the Lord God, 'who is and who was and who is to come, the Almighty (Revelation 1 ,8).' "

"When I saw him, I fell at his feet as though dead. But he laid his right hand upon me, saying, 'Fear not, I am the first and the last, and the living one; I died, and behold I am alive for evermore ... (Revelation 1,17-18).' "

"And he said to me, 'It is done! I am the Alpha and the Omega, the beginning and the end. To the thirsty I will give from the fountain of the water of life without payment (Revelation 21, 6).' "

The word for "first" is "protos," which means beginning or foremost and the word for "last" is "eschatos" which means farthest, last, or uttermost.

Musically, we are reminded of the beginning of an eleventh century plainsong, the Divinum Mysterium,

"Of the Father's love begotten,
Ere the worlds began to be,
He is Alpha and Omega,
He the source, the ending he …."

THE AMEN

"For the Son of God, Jesus Christ, whom we preached among you… was not Yes and No; but in him it is always Yes. For all the promises of God find their Yes in him. That is why we utter the Amen through him, to the glory of God (2 Corinthians 1,19-20)."

In the book of the Revelation, Jesus is referred to as "the Amen, the faithful and true witness, the beginning of God's creation (Revelation 3, 14)."

The Hebrew word "amen" is used in this verse as a verbal adjective which means firm, faithful, and trustworthy.

ANCIENT OF DAYS

"As I looked,
          thrones were placed
                and one that was ancient of days
                      took his seat;
his raiment was white as snow,
  and the hair of his head like pure wool;
this throne was fiery flames,
  its wheels were burning fire.
A stream of fire issued
  and came forth from before him;
a thousand thousands served him,
  and ten thousand times ten

thousand stood before him;
the court sat in judgment
and the books were opened.

I saw in the night visions,
and behold, with clouds of
   heaven
   there came one like a son of man,
and he came to the Ancient of Days
and was presented before him.
And to him was given dominion
and glory and kingdom,
that all peoples, nations, and
   languages
should serve him;
his dominion is an everlasting
   dominion,
   which shall not pass away,
and his kingdom one
   that shall not be destroyed.

... the Ancient of Days came, and judgment was given
for the saints of the Most High, and the time came when
the saints received the kingdom (Daniel 7, 9,10,13,14,22)."

APOSTLE

"... consider Jesus, the apostle and high priest
       of our confession (Hebrews 3,1)."

The word "apostle" is derived from the Greek word "apostolos," which means, a messenger, on this case, one who is sent forth with the Gospel of Christ.

AUTHOR

The Greek word here is "archegos" which means author, captain, or prince. The New American Bible and the New Jerusalem Bible translate "author" as "leader." The NRSV uses the word "pioneer."

"It was fitting that God, for whom and through whom all things exist, in bringing many children to glory, should make the pioneer of their salvation perfect through sufferings (Hebrews 2, 10 NRSV)."

"Therefore, since we are surrounded by so great a cloud of witnesses, let us also lay aside every weight and the sin that clings so closely, and let us run with perseverance the race that is before us, looking to Jesus the pioneer and perfecter of our faith, who for the sake of the joy that was set before him endured the cross, disregarding its shame, and has taken his seat at the right hand of the throne of God. Consider him who endured such hostility against himself from sinners, so that you may not grow weary or lose heart (Hebrews 12, 1-3 NRSV)."

BEGINNING

" '… The words of the Amen, the faithful and true witness, the beginning of God's creation (Revelation 3, 14).' "

The <u>New American Standard Bible</u> refers to "the Beginning" of the creation of God and the <u>New Jerusalem Bible</u> refers to " the Principle of God's creation."

The Greek word is "arche" meaning "the person or thing that commences, the first person or thing in a series, the leader." (Thayer's <u>Greek-English Lexicon of the New Testament</u>)

"He is before all things
    and in him all things hold together.
He is the head of the body, the church;
he is the beginning, the first-born from the dead,
    that in everything he might be preeminent
        (Colossians 1, 17-18)."

" 'I am the Alpha and the Omega, the beginning and the end (Revelation 21, 6).' "

Again, in the last chapter of the book of the Revelation of St. John, Jesus is called the Beginning.
" 'I am the Alpha and the Omega,
    the first and the last,
        the beginning and the end.
I Jesus have sent my angel to you with this testimony
        for the churches (Revelation 13, 16a).' "

BISHOP

"For ye were as sheep going astray;
    but are now returned unto

the Shepherd and Bishop of your souls (1 Peter 2, 25 KJV)."

The Greek word here is "episkopos" which means overseer, superintendent, or a guardian of souls.

Jesus, our Good Shepherd, is carefully guarding us on our pilgrimage to the house of our Father.

BRANCH

"There shall come forth a shoot
    from the stump of Jesse,
and a branch shall grow out of his roots.
And the Spirit of the LORD shall
    rest upon him,
the spirit of wisdom and
    understanding,
the spirit of counsel and might,
the spirit of knowledge and the
    fear of the LORD.
And his delight shall be in the fear
    of the LORD (Isaiah 11, 1-2)."

" 'Behold, the days are coming, says the LORD, when I will raise up for David a righteous Branch, and he shall reign as king and deal wisely, and shall execute justice and righteousness in the land. In his days Judah will be saved, and Israel will dwell securely. And this is the name by which he will be called: 'The LORD is our righteousness.'
(Jeremiah 23, 5).' "

" 'In those days and at that time I will cause a righteous Branch to spring forth for David; and he shall execute justice and righteousness in the land. In those days Judah will be saved and Jerusalem will dwell securely. And this is the name by which it shall be called: 'The LORD is our righteousness (Jeremiah 33, 15).' "

BREAD OF LIFE

"Jesus then said to them, 'Truly, truly, I say to you, it was not Moses who gave you the bread of heaven; my Father gives you the true bread from heaven. For the bread of God is that which comes down from heaven, and gives his life to the world.' They said to him, 'Lord, give us this bread always.'

Jesus said to them, 'I am the bread of life; he who comes to me shall not hunger, and he who believes in me shall never thirst.'

'I am the bread of life. Your fathers ate the manna in the wilderness, and they died. This is the bread which comes down from heaven, that a man may eat of it and not die.

I am the living bread which came down from heaven; if any one eats of this bread, he will live for ever; and the bread which I shall give for the life of the world is my flesh (John 6, 32-35,48-51).' "

"The Jews then disputed among themselves, saying, 'How can this man give us his flesh to eat?' So Jesus said to them, 'Truly, truly, I say to you, unless you eat the flesh of the Son of man and drink his blood, you have no life in you; he who eats my flesh and drinks my blood has eternal life, and I will raise him up at the last day. For my flesh is food indeed, and my blood is drink indeed. He who eats my flesh and drinks my blood abides in me, and I in him. As the living Father sent me, and I live because of the Father, so he who eats me will live because of me. This is the bread which came down from heaven, not such as the fathers ate and died; he who eats this bread will live for ever (John 6, 52-58).' "

"Jesus, full of the Holy Spirit, returned from the Jordan and was led by the Spirit in the wilderness, where for forty days he was tempted by the devil. He ate nothing at all during those days, and when they were over, he was famished. The devil said to him, 'If you are the Son of God, command this stone to become a loaf of bread.' Jesus answered him, 'It is written, 'One does not live by bread alone (Luke 4, 1-4 NRSV).' "

At the Last Supper, Jesus "... took bread, and when he had given thanks he broke it and gave it to them, saying, 'This is my body which is given for you. Do this in remembrance of me.' And likewise the cup after supper, saying, 'This cup which is poured out for you is the new covenant in my blood (Luke 22, 19, 20).' "

Saint Paul writes, "For I received from the Lord what I also handed on to you, that the Lord Jesus on the night when he was betrayed took a loaf of bread, and when he had given thanks, he broke it and said, 'This is my body that is for you. Do this in remembrance of me.' In the same way he took the cup also, after supper, saying, 'This cup is the new covenant in my blood. Do this, as often as you drink it, in remembrance of me.' For as often as you eat this bread and drink the cup, you proclaim the Lord's death until he comes. Whoever therefore eats the bread or drinks the cup of the Lord in an unworthy manner will be answerable for the body and blood of the Lord. Examine yourselves, and only then eat of the bread and drink of the cup. For all who eat and drink without discerning the body, eat and drink judgment against themselves (1 Corinthians 11, 23-29 NRSV)."

"The cup of blessing that we bless, is it not a sharing in the blood of Christ? The bread that we break, is it not a sharing in the body of Christ? Because there is one bread, we who are many are one body, for we all partake of the one bread (1 Corinthians 19, 16-17 NRSV)."

The word "remembrance" in 1 Corinthians 11, 24 is "anamnesis." This is not just a casual word as in, "Oh yeah, I remember that."

This word "anamnesis" reminds us that God's saving actions become PRESENT to us right here, right now.

Please consult the <u>Catechism of the Catholic Church</u> (available online) to learn more about the sacrament of the Eucharist. See Part Two, Article 3)

BRIDEGROOM

"And Jesus said to them, 'Can you make wedding guests fast while the bridegroom is with them? The days will come, when the bridegroom is taken away from them, and then they will fast in those days (Luke 5, 34,35).'"

Here is the beautiful imagery of Christ as the bridegroom and the Church as the bride. This is foreshadowed in the Old Testament where God "marries," or enters into a covenant relationship with the nation of Israel.

"... I plighted my troth to you and entered into a covenant with you, says the LORD God, and you became mine." (Ezekiel 16, 8b). "... as the bridegroom rejoices over the bride, so shall your God rejoice over you (Isaiah 62, 5b)."

" 'And in that day, says the LORD, you will call me, 'My husband.... And I will betroth you to me for ever; I will betroth you to me in righteousness and in justice, in steadfast love, and in mercy. I will betroth you to me in faithfulness; and you shall know the LORD (Hosea 2, 16a, 19,20).'"

In all three synoptic Gospels, Jesus refers to Himself as the "bridegroom." The question involved was one of fasting. At the feast at the house of Levi (Matthew), Jesus was asked,

" 'Why do you eat and drink with tax collectors and sinners?' And Jesus answered them, 'Those who are well have no need of a physician, but those who are sick; I have not come to call the righteous, but sinners to repentance.' And they said to him, 'The disciples of John fast often and offer prayers, and so do the disciples of the Pharisees, but yours eat and drink.' And Jesus said to them, 'Can you make wedding guests fast while the bridegroom is with them? The days will come when the bridegroom is taken away from them, and then they will fast in those days (Luke 5, 30b-35).' "

In the Gospel of John, Jesus is referred to as the "bridegroom" by John the Baptist, who said, " '... I am not the Christ, but I have been sent before him. He who has the bride is the bridegroom; the friend of the bridegroom, who stands and hears him, rejoices greatly at the bridegroom's voice; therefore this joy of mine is now full. He must increase, but I must decrease (John 3, 28b-30).' "

BROTHER

"While he was still speaking to the people, behold, his mother and his brothers stood outside, asking to speak to him. But he replied to the man who told him, 'Who is my mother, and who are my brothers? And stretching out his hand towards his disciples, he said, 'Here are my mother and my brothers! For whoever does the will of my Father in heaven is my brother, and sister, and mother (Matthew 12, 46-50).' " Parallel passages are in Mark and Luke.

Jesus, our Brother, will be our judge. How we treat other followers of Jesus is of crucial importance.

"When the Son of Man comes in his glory, and all the angels with him, then he will sit on his glorious throne. Before him will be gathered all the nations, and he will separate them one from another as a shepherd separates the sheep from the goats, and he will place the sheep at his right hand, but the goats at the left. Then the King will say to those at his right hand, 'Come, O blessed of my Father, inherit the kingdom prepared for you from the foundation of the world; for

> I was hungry and you gave me food,
> I was thirsty and you gave me drink,
> I was a stranger and you welcomed me,
> I was naked and you clothed me,
> I was sick and you visited me,
> I was in prison and you came to me.'

Then the righteous will answer him,

> 'Lord, when did we see thee hungry and feed thee,
> or thirsty and give thee a drink?
> And when did we see thee a stranger and welcome thee,
> or naked and clothe thee?
> And when did we see thee sick
> or in prison
> and visit thee?'

And the King will answer them,

> 'Truly, I say to you, as you did it to one of the least of these
>
> my brethren,
>
> you did it to me (Matthew 25, 31-40).'"

"For it was fitting that he, for whom and by whom all things exist, in bringing many sons to glory, should make the pioneer of their salvation perfect through suffering. For he who sanctifies and those who are sanctified have all one origin. That is why he is not ashamed to call them brethren, saying,

> 'I will proclaim thy name to my brethren, in the midst
> of the congregation I will praise thee (Hebrews 2, 10-12).'"

"Since therefore the children share in flesh and blood, he himself likewise partook of the same nature, that through death he might destroy him who has the power of death, that is, the devil, and deliver all those who through fear of death were subject to life-long bondage. For surely it is not with angels that he is concerned but with the descendants of Abraham. Therefore he had to be made like his brethren in every respect, so that he might become a merciful and faithful high priest in the service of God, to make expiation for the sins of the people. For because he himself has suffered and been tempted, he is able to help those who are tempted (Hebrews 2, 14-18)."

CAPTAIN

"It was fitting that God, for whom and through whom all things exist, in bringing many children to glory, should make the pioneer of their salvation perfect through sufferings (Hebrew 2, 10 NRSV)."

In Hebrews 2, 10 (KJV), Jesus is referred to as the "captain of their salvation," whereas the NRSV uses the word "pioneer." The Greek word is "archegos" which means author, captain, or prince.

CHILD

"For to us a child is born,
 to us a son is given;
 and the government will be upon his shoulder,
 and his name will be called
'Wonderful Counselor,
   Mighty God,
     Everlasting Father,
       Prince of Peace (Isaiah 9, 6)."

This is a prophecy of the coming of the Messianic King.

"Now when Jesus was born in Bethlehem of Judea in the days of Herod the king, behold, wise men from the East came to Jerusalem, saying, 'Where is he who has been born king of the Jews? For we have seen his star in the East, and have come to worship him.' When Herod the king heard this, he was troubled, and all Jerusalem with him; and assembling all the chief priests and scribes of the people, he inquired of them where the Christ was to be born. They told him, 'In Bethlehem of Judea; for so it is written by the prophet:

'And you, O Bethlehem, in the land
  of Judah,
 are by no means least among the
  rulers of Judah;
 for from you shall come a ruler
 who will govern my people
  Israel.'

Then Herod summoned the wise men secretly and ascertained from them what time the star appeared; and he sent them to Bethlehem, saying, 'Go and search diligently for the child, and when you have found him bring me word, that I too may come and worship him.' When they had heard the king they went their way; and lo, the star which they had seen in the East went before them, till it came to rest over the place where the child was. When they saw the star, they rejoiced exceedingly with great joy; and going into the house they saw the child with Mary his mother, and they fell down and worshipped him. Then, opening their treasures, they offered him gifts, gold and frankincense and myrrh (Matthew 2, 1-11)."

"And when the time came for their purification according to the law of Moses, they brought him up to Jerusalem to present him to the Lord (as it is written in the law of the Lord, 'Every male that openeth the womb shall be called holy to the Lord') and to offer a sacrifice according to what is said in the law of the Lord, 'a pair of turtledoves, or two young pigeons.' Now there was a man in Jerusalem, whose name was Simeon, and this man was righteous and devout, looking for the consolation of Israel, and the Holy Spirit was upon him. And it had been revealed to him by the Holy Spirit that he should not see death before he had seen the Lord's Christ. And inspired by the Spirit he came to the temple; and when the parents brought in the child Jesus, to do for him according to the custom of the law, he took him up in his arms and blessed God and said,

> 'Lord, now lettest thou thy servant
>   depart in peace,
> according to thy word;
> for mine eyes have seen thy
>   salvation
> which thou hast prepared in the
>   presence of all the peoples,
> a light for revelation to the Gentiles,
> and for glory to thy people Israel.'

And his father and mother marveled at what was said about him; and Simeon blessed them and said to Mary his mother,

> 'Behold, this child is set for the fall
>   and rising of many in Israel,
> and for a sign that is spoken against
> (and a sword will pierce through
>   your own soul also),
> that thoughts out of many hearts may
>   be revealed (Luke 2, 22-35).' "

"And when they had performed everything according to the law of the Lord, they returned into Galilee, to their own city, Nazareth. And the child grew and became strong, filled with wisdom; and the favor of God was upon him (Luke 2, 39-40)."

"... behold, an angel of the Lord appeared to Joseph in a dream and said, 'Rise, take the child and his mother, and flee to Egypt, and remain there till I tell you; for Herod is about to search for the child, to destroy him.' And he rose and took the child and his mother by night, and departed to Egypt, and remained there until the death of Herod. This was to fulfil what the Lord had spoken by the prophet, 'Out of Egypt have I called my son (Matthew 2, 13-15).' "

"... thy holy child Jesus ... (Acts 4, 27,30 KJV) (Jesus is referred to as a child, or a servant, in this prayer of Peter and John)."

CHRIST (MESSIAH)

The Greek word here is "Christos," which means "Messiah" or "anointed."

Andrew, the fisherman, "... first found his brother Simon, and said to him, 'We have found the Messiah (which means Christ) John 1, 41.'"

"Now when Jesus came into the district of Caesarea Philippi, he asked his disciples, 'Who do people say that the Son of man is?' And they said, 'Some say John the Baptist, but others Elijah, and still others Jeremiah or one of the prophets.' He said to them,

'But who do you say that I am?'

Simon Peter answered, 'You are the Messiah, the son of the living God.'

And Jesus answered him, 'Blessed are you, Simon son of Jonah! For flesh and blood has not revealed this to you, but my Father in heaven. And I tell you, you are Peter, and on this rock I will build my church, and the gates of Hades will not prevail against it. I will give you the keys of the kingdom of heaven, and whatever you bind on earth will be bound in heaven, and whatever you loose on earth will be loosed in heaven (Matthew 16, 13-19 NRSV).'"

During the conversation Jesus had with the woman at the well, she said to Him, " 'I know that Messiah is coming (he who is called Christ); when he comes, he will show us all things.' Jesus said to her,

'I who speak to you am he.'

Just then his disciples came. They marveled that he was talking to a woman, but none said, 'What do you wish?' or, 'Why are you talking with her?' So the woman left with her water jar, and went away into the city, and said to the people,

'Come, see a man who told me all I ever did. Can this be the Christ? (John 4, 25-29).'"

Jesus often visited his friends, Mary, Martha and their brother Lazarus in a town called Bethany. After the death and burial of Lazarus,

Jesus said to Martha, " '... Your brother will rise again.' Martha said to him, 'I know that he will rise again in the resurrection on the last day.' Jesus said to her, 'I am the resurrection and the life. Those who believe in me, even though they die, will live, and everyone who lives and believes in me will never die. Do you believe this? She said to him,

> 'Yes, Lord, I believe that you are the Messiah, the
> Son of God, the one coming into this world
> (John 11, 23b-27).' "

"Now when the sun was setting, all those who had any that were sick with various diseases brought them to him; and he laid his hands on every one of them and healed them. And demons also came out of many, crying, 'You are the Son of God!' But he rebuked them, and would not allow them to speak, because they knew that he was the Christ (Luke 4, 40-41)."

> "Christ, our paschal lamb, has been sacrificed.
> Let us, therefore, celebrate the festival,
> not with the old leaven of malice and evil,
> but with the unleavened bread of sincerity and truth
> (1 Corinthians 5, 7b-8)."

"... Christ our passover is sacrificed for us: Therefore let us keep the feast. not with old leaven, neither with the leaven of malice and wickedness; but with the unleavened bread of sincerity and truth (1 Corinthians 5, 7b-8 KJV)."

COUNSELOR

In Jesus' farewell discourse to his followers, he said,

"If you love me, you will keep my commandments. And I will pray the Father, and he will give you another Counselor, to be with you for ever, even the Spirit of truth, whom the world cannot receive, because it neither sees him nor knows him; you know him, for he dwells with you, and will be in you (John 14,15-17)."

The Greek word we are studying here is "parakletos," which means intercessor, consoler, advocate, and comforter. The Holy Spirit is right here to help us.

"... the Counselor, the Holy Spirit, whom the Father will receive in my name, he will teach you all things, and bring to your remembrance all that I have said to you (John 14, 26)."

"... when the Counselor comes, whom I shall send to you from the Father, even the Spirit of truth, who proceeds from the Father, he will bear witness to me ... (John 15, 26)."

"... it is to your advantage that I go away, for if I do not go away, the Counselor will not come to you; but if I go, I will send him to you. And when he comes, he will convince the world concerning sin and righteousness and judgment: concerning sin, because they do not believe in me; concerning righteousness, because I go to the Father, and you will see me no more; concerning judgement, because the ruler of this world is judged (John 16, 7)."

There are numerous Old Testament passages about the Lord being our counselor:

"I bless the LORD who gives me counsel;
in the night also my heart instructs me (Psalm 16, 7)."

"I will instruct you and teach you
the way you should go;
I will counsel you with my eye upon you (Psalm 32, 8)."

"The counsel of the LORD stands for ever,
the thoughts of his heart to all generations (Psalm 33, 11)."

"Nevertheless I am continually with thee;
thou dost hold my right hand.
Thou dost guide me with thy counsel,
and afterward thou wilt receive me to glory (Psalm 73, 23-24)."

"But they soon forgot his works;
they did not wait for his counsel.
But they had a wanton craving in the wilderness,
and put God to the test in the desert;
he gave them what they asked,
but sent a wasting disease among them (Psalm 106, 13-15)."

This psalm recounts God's great
deeds of delivering the Israelites out of Egypt.
There are references to the continual rebellion
on the part of Israel.

"Some sat in darkness and in gloom.
prisoners in affliction and in irons,

for they had rebelled against the
words of God,
and spurned the counsel of the
Most High (Psalm 107, 10-11)."

"Because I called and you refused to listen,
have stretched out my hand and no one has heeded,
and you have ignored all my counsel
and would have none of my reproof,
I also will laugh at your calamity;
I will mock when panic strikes you,
when panic strikes you like a storm,
and calamity comes like a whirlwind,
when distress and anguish come upon you.
Then they will call upon me, but I will not answer;
they will seek me diligently but will not find me.
Because they hated knowledge
and did not choose the fear of the LORD,
and would have none of my counsel,
and despised all my reproof,
therefore they shall eat the fruit of their way
and be sated with their own devices (Proverbs 1, 24-31)."

"Thy testimonies are my delight,
   they are my counselors (Psalm 119, 24)."

"I have counsel and sound wisdom,
   I have insight, I have strength(Proverb 8, 14)."

Wisdom, personified, is speaking in this verse.

"... the LORD of hosts ...is wonderful in counsel,
   and excellent in wisdom (Isaiah 28, 29)."

"Who has directed the Spirit of the LORD,
   or as his counselor has instructed him (Isaiah 40, 13)?"

"... O great and mighty God whose name is the LORD of hosts,
   great in counsel and mighty in deed ...
               (Jeremiah 32, 18c-19a)."

"For to us a child is born,
to us a son is given;
and the government shall be upon his shoulder,
and his name will be called

'Wonderful Counselor,
Mighty God,
Everlasting Father,
Prince of Peace (Isaiah 9, 6).' "

CREATOR

The following verses are, by necessity, only a sampling of the multitude of verses which refer to God as Creator.

"In the beginning God created the heavens and the earth. The earth was without form and void, and darkness was upon the face of the deep; and the Spirit of God was moving over the face of the waters.

And God said, 'Let there be light', and there was light. And God saw that the light was good; and God separated the light from the darkness. God called the light Day, and the darkness he called Night. And there was evening and there was morning, one day

And God said, 'Let there be a firmament in the midst of the waters, and let it separate the waters from the waters.' And God made the firmament and separated the waters which were under the firmament from the waters which were above the firmament. And it was so. And God called the firmament Heaven. And there was evening and there was morning, a second day.

And God said, 'Let the waters under the heavens be gathered together into one place, and let the dry land appear.' And it was so. God called the dry land Earth, and the waters that were gathered together he called Seas. And God saw that it was good. And God said, 'Let the earth put forth vegetation, plants yielding seeds, and fruit trees bearing fruit in which is their seed, each according to its kind, upon the earth.' And it was so. The earth brought forth vegetation, plants yielding seed according to their own kinds, and trees bearing fruit in which is their seed, each according to its kind. And God saw that it was good. And there was evening and there was morning, a third day.

And God said, 'Let there be lights in the firmament of the heavens to separate the day from the night; and let them be for signs and for seasons and for days and years, and let them be lights in the firmament of the heavens to give light upon the earth.' And it was so. And God made the two great lights, the greater light to rule the day, and the lesser light to rule the night; he made the stars also. And God set them in the firmament of the heavens to give light upon the earth, to rule over the day and over the night, and to separate the light from the darkness. And God saw that it was good. And there was evening and there was morning, a fourth day.

And God said, 'Let the waters bring forth swarms of living creatures, and let the birds fly above the earth across the firmament of the heavens.' So God created the great sea monsters and every living creature that moves, with which the waters swarm, according to their kinds, and every winged bird according to its kind. And God saw that it was good. And God blessed them, saying, 'Be fruitful and multiply and fill the waters in the seas, and let the birds multiply on the earth.' And there was evening and there was morning, a fifth day.

And God said, 'Let the earth bring forth living creatures according to their kinds: cattle and creeping things and beasts of the earth according to their kinds.' And it was so. And God made the beasts of the earth according to their kinds and the cattle according to their kinds, and everything that creeps upon the ground according to its kind. And God saw that it was good.

Then God said, 'Let us make man in our image, after our likeness; and let them have dominion over the fish of the sea, and over the birds of the air, and over the cattle, and over all the earth, and over every creeping thing that creeps upon the earth.' So God created man in his own image, in the image of God he created him; male and female he created them. And God blessed them, and God said to them, 'Be fruitful and multiply, and fill the earth and subdue it; and have dominion over the fish of the sea and over the birds of the air and over every living thing that moves upon the earth.' And God said, 'Behold, I have given you every plant yielding seed which is upon the face of all the earth, and every tree with seed in its fruit; you shall have them for food. And to every beast of the earth, and to every bird of the air, and to everything that creeps upon the earth, everything that has the breath of life, I have given every green plant for food.' And it was so. And God saw everything that he had made, and behold, it was very good. And there as evening and there was morning, a sixth day (Genesis 1,1-31)."

Adam! "When God created humankind, he made them in the likeness of God. Male and female he created them, and he blessed them and named them 'Humankind' when they were created (Genesis 5, 1b-2 NRSV)." The Hebrew word for "humankind" is "adam."

"O LORD, how manifold are thy works!
In wisdom hast thou made them all;
the earth is full of thy creatures (Psalm 104, 24)."

Psalm 104 as a whole praises God as Creator.

"Praise the LORD!
 Praise the LORD from the heavens,
 praise him in the heights!
 Praise him, all his angels,
 praise him, all his host!

Praise him, sun and moon,
    praise him, all you shining stars!
Praise him, you highest heavens,
    and you waters above the heavens!

Let them praise the name of the LORD!
For he commanded and they were created.
And he established them for ever and ever;
he fixed their bounds which cannot be passed.

Praise the LORD from the earth,
    you sea monsters and all deeps,
fire and hail, snow and frost,
    stormy wind fulfilling his command!

Mountains and all hills,
    fruit trees and all cedars!
Beasts and all cattle,
    creeping things and flying birds!

Kings of the earth and all peoples,
    princes and all rulers of the earth!
Young men and maidens together,
    old men and children!

Let them praise the name of the LORD,
for his name alone is exalted;
his glory is above earth and heaven.
He has raised up a horn for his people,
praise for all his saints,
for the people of Israel who are near to him.
Praise the LORD (Psalm 148, 1-14)!"

"Remember your Creator in the days of your youth ...
                    (Ecclesiastes 12, 1a)"

"To whom then will you compare me,
  that I should be like him? says the Holy One?
Lift up your eyes on high and see:
  who created these?
He who brings out their host by number,
  calling them all by name;
by the greatness of his might,
  and because he is strong in power
not one is missing (Isaiah 40, 25-26)."

"When the poor and needy seek water, and there is none, and their tongue is parched with thirst, I the LORD will answer them, I the God of Israel will not forsake them. I will open rivers on the bare heights, and fountains in the midst of the valleys; I will make the wilderness a pool of water, and the dry land springs of water. I will put in the wilderness the cedar, the acacia, the myrtle, and the olive; I will set in the desert the cypress, the plane and the pine together, so that all may see and know, all may consider and understand, that the hand of the LORD has done this, the Holy One of Israel has created it (Isaiah 41, 17-20 NRSV)."

"Thus says God, the LORD,
  who created the heavens and stretched them out,
who spread forth the earth and what comes from it,
who gives breath to the people upon it
  and spirit to those who walk in it … (Isaiah 42, 5)."

"I am the LORD, your Holy One,
  the Creator of Israel, your King."
'Remember not the former things,
  nor consider the things of old.
Behold, I am doing a new thing;
  now it springs forth, do you not perceive it?
I will make a way in the wilderness
  and rivers in the desert.
The jackals and the ostriches;
  for I give water in the wilderness,
  rivers in the desert'
to give drink to my chosen people,
  the people whom I formed for myself
that they might declare my praise." (Isaiah 43, 15, 18-21)."

"I am the LORD, and there is no other,
 I form light and I create darkness,
 I make weal and create woe;
 I, the LORD, do all these things.

> Shower, O heavens, from above,
>> and let the skies rain down righteousness;
> let the earth open, that salvation may spring up,
>> and let it cause righteousness to sprout up also;
> I the LORD have created it.

Woe to you who strive with your Maker, earthen vessels with the potter! Does the clay say to the one who fashions it, 'What are you making'? or 'Your work has no handles'? Woe to anyone who says to a father, 'What are you begetting?' or to a woman, 'With what are you in labor.' I made the earth, and created humankind upon it; it was my hands that stretched out the heavens, and I commanded all their host. For thus says the LORD, who created the heavens (he is God!) who formed the earth, and made it (he established it; he did not create it a chaos, he formed it to be inhabited.)!" I am the LORD, and there is no other (Isaiah 45, 6c-10, 12, 18 NRSV)."

> "For I will not contend for ever,
>> nor will I always be angry;
> for from me proceeds the spirit,
>> and I have made the breath of life (Isaiah 57, 16)."

> " 'For behold, I create new heavens and a new earth;
>> and the former things shall not be remembered
> or come into mind.
>
> But be glad and rejoice for ever
>> in that which I create;
> for behold, I create Jerusalem a rejoicing,
>> and her people a joy (Isaiah 65, 17,18).' "

"For lo, the one who forms the mountains, creates the wind, reveals his thoughts to mortals, makes the morning darkness, and treads on the heights of the earth – the LORD, the God of hosts, is his name (Amos 4, 13 NRSV)."

Jesus said, " 'But from the beginning of creation, God made them male and female.' For this reason a man shall leave his father and mother and be joined to his wife, and the two shall become one flesh. So they are no longer two, but one flesh. Therefore what God has joined together, let no one separate (Mark 10, 6-9 NRSV)."

"Ever since the creation of the world his invisible nature, namely his eternal power and deity, has been clearly perceived in the things that have been made (Romans 1, 20a)."

"We know that the whole creation has been groaning in labor pains until now; and not only the creation, but we ourselves, who have the first fruits of the Spirit, groan inwardly while we wait for adoption, the redemption of our bodies (Romans 8, 22-23 NRSV)."

"We are what he has made us, created in Christ Jesus for good works, which God prepared beforehand to be our way of life (Ephesians 2, 10 NRSV)."

"Although I am the very least of all the saints, this grace was given to me to bring to the Gentiles the news of the boundless riches of Christ, and to make everyone see what is the plan of the mystery hidden for ages in God who created all things (Ephesians 3, 8, 9 NRSV).

"Put off your old nature which belongs to your former manner of life and is corrupt through deceitful lusts, and be renewed in the spirit of your minds, and put on the new nature, created after the likeness of God in true righteousness and holiness (Ephesians 4, 22-24)."

"He is the image of the invisible God, the first-born of all creation; for in him all things were created, in heaven and on earth, visible and invisible, whether thrones or dominions or principalities or authorities -- all things were created through him and for him. He is before all things, and in him all things hold together (Colossians 1, 15-17)."

"Do not lie to each other, seeing that you have stripped off the old self with its practices and have clothed yourselves with the new self, which is being renewed in knowledge according to the image of its creator. In that renewal there is no longer Greek and Jew, circumcised and uncircumcised, barbarian, Scythian, slave and free; but Christ is all and in all (Colossians 3, 9-11 NRSV)."

"For everything created by God is good, and nothing is to be rejected if it is received with thanksgiving; for then it is consecrated by the word of God and prayer (1 Timothy 4, 4-5)."

"Therefore let those who suffer according to God's will do right and entrust their souls to a faithful Creator (1 Peter 4,19)."

Jesus is referred to as "... the Amen,
    the faithful and true witness,
        the beginning of God's creation (Revelation 3, 14)."

The heavenly chorus sings God's praises:

" 'You are worthy, our Lord and God,
   to receive glory and honor and power,
   or you created all things, and
   by your will they existed and were created
                             (Revelations 4, 11 NRSV).' "

DELIVERER

"... the LORD said, 'I have seen the affliction of my people who are in Egypt, and have heard their cry because of their taskmasters; I know their sufferings, and I have come down to deliver them ot the hand of the Egyptians, and to bring them up out of that land to a good and broad land, a land flowing with milk and honey... (Exodus 3, 7-8).' "

David, before slaying Goliath, says to King Saul,

" 'The LORD who delivered me from the paw of the lion
   and from the paw of the bear, will deliver me from the
   hand of this Philistine (1 Samuel 17, 37).' "

      God's people have always found strength and courage
      to face their challenges by recalling God's faithfulness
      in past difficulties.

Later, David "... spoke to the LORD the words of this song on the day when the LORD delivered him from the hand of all his enemies and from the hand of Saul. He said,

'The LORD is my rock, and my fortress, and my deliverer,
my God, my rock, in whom I take refuge,
my shield and the horn of my salvation,
my stronghold and my refuge,
my savior; thou savest me from violence.

I call upon the LORD, who is worthy to be praised,
and I am saved from my enemies (2 Samuel 22, 1-4).' "

(The word "deliverer" is "palat" which means
       "to carry away safe.")

God "... delivers the afflicted by their affliction,
       and opens their ear by adversity (Job 36, 15)."

(The speaker is Elihu. He was the only one
of Job's "friends" not rebuked by God).

"I love thee, O LORD, my strength.
The LORD is my rock, and my fortress, and my deliverer,
my God, my rock, in whom I take refuge,
my shield, and the horn of my salvation, my stronghold.

In my distress I called upon the LORD;
to my God I cried for help.

From his temple he heard my voice,
and my cry to him reached his ears.

He reached from on high,
he took me,
he drew me out of many waters.
He delivered me from my strong enemy
and from those who hated me;
for they were too mighty for me.
They came upon me in the day of my calamity;
but the LORD was my stay.

He brought me forth into a broad place;
He delivered me because he delighted in me
              (Psalm 18, 1, 6, 16-19)."

"You are a hiding place for me;
  you preserve me from trouble;
  you surround me with glad cries
of deliverance (Psalm 32, 7)."

"I sought the LORD, and he answered me
and delivered me from all my fears.
Look to him, and be radiant;
so your faces shall never be ashamed.
This poor soul cried, and was heard by the LORD,
and was saved from every trouble.
The angel of the LORD encamps around those
who fear him, and delivers them.
O taste and see that the LORD is good; happy are those
who take refuge in him. Many are the afflictions of the righteous,
but the LORD rescues them from all their troubles
              (Psalm 34, 4-8, 19 NRSV)."

"As for me, I am poor and needy;
 but the LORD takes thought for me.
 You are my help and my deliverer;
 do not delay, O my God (Psalm 40,17 NRSV)!"

"Happy are those who consider the poor;
 The LORD delivers them in the day of trouble
                             (Psalm 41,1 NRSV)."

"With a freewill offering I will
sacrifice to you;
I will give thanks to your name,
O LORD, for it is good.
For he has delivered me from
every trouble,
and my eye has looked in
triumph on my enemies (Psalm 54, 6-7 NRSV)."

"But as for me, my prayer is to you, O LORD.
At an acceptable time, O God,
in the abundance of your
    steadfast love, answer me.
With your faithful help rescue
    me
from sinking in the mire;
let me be delivered from my
    enemies.
and from the deep waters (Psalm 69, 13-14 NRSV)."

"Help us, O God of our salvation,
    for the glory of your name;
deliver us, and forgive our sins,
    for your name's sake (Psalm 79, 9 NRSV)."

"You who live in the shelter of the Most High, who abide in the shadow of the Almighty, will say to the LORD, 'My refuge and my fortress; my God, in whom I put my trust.' For he will deliver you from the snare of the fowler and from the deadly pestilence; he will cover you with his pinions, and under his wings you will find refuge; his faithfulness is a shield and buckler (Psalm 91, 1-4 NRSV)."

"Many times he delivered them,
    but they were rebellious in their purposes,
    and were brought low through their iniquity (Psalm 106, 43)."

"Then they cried to the LORD in their trouble,

and he delivered them from their distress;
he sent forth his word and healed them,
and delivered them from destruction (Psalm 107, 19-20)."

"Return, O my soul, to your rest,
  for the LORD has dealt
    bountifully with you.
 For you have delivered my soul
    from death,
  my eyes from tears,
  my feet from stumbling.
I walk before the LORD
  in the land of the living (Psalm 116, 7-9 NRSV)."

"Deliver me, O LORD, from my enemies!
 I have fled to thee for refuge (Psalm 143,8)."

"Blessed be the LORD, my rock,
  who trains my hands for war,
    and my fingers for battle;
my rock and my fortress,
  my stronghold and my
    deliverer,
my shield, in whom I take refuge,
  who subdues the peoples under
    me.
Stretch out your hand from on
  high;
set me free and rescue me from
  the mighty waters (Psalm 144, 1, 2, 7 NRSV)."

"I am God, and also henceforth I am He;
 there is no one who can deliver from my hand;
 I work and who can hinder it (Isaiah 43,13 NRSV)."

"Now the word of the LORD came to me saying,
'Before I formed you in the
  womb I knew you,
and before you were born I
  consecrated you;
I appointed you a prophet to the
  nations.
Do not be afraid of them,
for I am with you to deliver you,
    says the LORD,
They will fight against you;

but they shall not prevail against you, for
I am with you, says the LORD, to deliver
you (Jeremiah 1, 4,5,8,19 NRSV).' "

"And I will make you to this people
    a fortified wall of bronze;
they will fight against you,
    but they shall not prevail over you,
for I am with you
to save and deliver you
    says the LORD.
I will deliver you out of the hand of the wicked,
    and redeem you from the grasp of the ruthless
        (Jeremiah 15, 20-21)."

"For thus says the LORD God, I myself will search for my sheep, and will seek them out. As shepherds seek out their flocks when they are among their scattered sheep, so I will seek out my sheep. I will rescue them from all the places to which they have been scattered on a day of clouds and thick darkness. I will bring them out from the peoples and gather them from the countries, and bring them into their own land; and I will feed them on the mountains of Israel, by the watercourses, and in all the inhabited parts of the land. I will feed them with good pasture.... I myself will be the shepherd of my sheep (Ezekiel 34, 11-14a,15a NRSV)."

Remember Daniel's three friends and the threat of the fiery furnace? "Shadrach, Meshach, and Abednego answered the king, 'O Nebuchadnessar, we have no need to answer you in this matter. If it be so, our God whom we serve is able to deliver us out of your hand, O king. But if not, be it known to you, O king, that we will not serve your gods or worship the golden image which you have set up (Daniel 3, 16-17).' " These three men were thrown into the fiery furnace and were indeed rescued by God.

Another king, Darius, decreed that Daniel be thrown into the lions' den. "Then, at break of day, the king arose and went in haste to the den of lions. When he came near to the den where Daniel was, he cried out in a tone of anguish and said to Daniel, 'O Daniel, servant of the living God, has your God, whom you serve continually, been able to deliver you from the lions?' Then Daniel said to the king, 'O king, live for ever! My God sent his angel and shut the lions' mouths, and they have not hurt me, because I was found blameless before him; and also before you, O king, I have done no wrong (Daniel 6,19-22).' "

"Then King Darius wrote to all peoples and nations of every

language, throughout the whole world:

> 'May you have abundant prosperity! I make a decree,
> that in all my royal dominion people should tremble
> and fear before the God of Daniel: For he is
> the living God, enduring forever. His kingdom shall
> never be destroyed, and his dominion has no end.
> He delivers and rescues, he works signs and wonders
> in heaven and on earth; for he has saved Daniel from
> the power of the lions (Daniel 6, 25-27 NRSV)."

"... all who call upon the name of the LORD shall be delivered (Joel 2, 32a)."

Jesus said, " 'Pray then in this way:

> Our Father in heaven, hallowed be your name.
> Your kingdom come. Your will be done, on earth
> as it is in heaven. Give us this day our daily bread.
> And forgive us our debts, as we have also forgiven our debtors.
> And do not bring us to the time of trial,
> but rescue us from the evil one.
>
> For if you forgive others their trespasses,
> your heavenly Father will also forgive you;
> but if you do not forgive others,
> neither will your Father forgive your trespasses
> (Matthew 6, 9-15NRSV).' "

"Wretched man that I am! Who will deliver me from this body of death? Thanks be to God through Jesus Christ our Lord (Romans 7, 24-25a)!"

"Lest you be wise in your own conceits, I want you to understand this mystery, brethren: a hardening has come upon part of Israel, until the full number of the Gentiles come in, and so all Israel will be saved; as it is written,

> 'The Deliverer will come from Zion,
> he will banish ungodliness from Jacob';
> 'and this will be my covenant with them
> when I take away their sins (Romans 11, 25-27).' "

"For we do not want you to be ignorant, brethren, of the affliction we experienced in Asia; for we were so utterly, unbearably crushed that we despaired of life itself. Why, we felt that we had received the sentence

of death itself; but that was to make us rely not on ourselves but on God who raises the dead; he delivered us from so deadly a peril, and he will deliver us; on him we have set our hope that he will deliver us again. You must also help us by prayer, so that many will give thanks on our behalf for the blessings granted us in answer to many prayers
(2 Corinthians 1, 8-11)."

"Grace to you and peace from God our Father and from the Lord Jesus Christ, who gave himself for our sins to deliver us from the present evil age, according to the will of our God and Father; and to whom be the glory for ever and ever. Amen. (Galatians 1,3-5)."

St. Paul wrote to the Colossians "... we have not ceased to pray for you, asking that you may be filled with the knowledge of his will in all spiritual wisdom and understanding, to lead a life worthy of the Lord, fully pleasing to him, bearing fruit in every good work and increasing in the knowledge of God. May you be strengthened with all power, according to his glorious might, for all endurance and patience with joy, giving thanks to the Father, who has qualified us to share in the inheritance of the saints in light. He has delivered us from the dominion of darkness and transferred us to the kingdom of his beloved Son, in whom we have redemption, the forgiveness of sins (Colossians 1, 9-14)."

"... you turned to God from idols, to serve a living and true God, and to wait for his Son from heaven, whom he raised from the dead, Jesus who delivers us from the wrath to come (1 Thessalonians 1, 9b-10)."

St. Paul wrote "Persecutions, afflictions ... what persecutions I endured: but out of them all the Lord delivered me
(2 Timothy 3, 10 KJV)."

"Since therefore the children share in flesh and blood, he himself likewise partook of the same nature, that through death he might destroy him who has the power of death, that is, the devil, and deliver all those who through fear of death were subject to lifelong bondage (Hebrews 2, 14-15)."

DOOR (also see "GATE")

"So Jesus again said to them, 'Truly. truly I say to you, I am the door of the sheep. All who came before me were thieves and robbers; but the sheep did not heed them. I am the door; if any one enters by me, he will be saved, and will go in and out and find pasture (John 10,7-9)."

EL-BETHEL (The God of Bethel)

"And Jacob came to Luz (that is, Bethel), which is in the land of Canaan, he and all the people who were with him, and there he built an altar, and called the place El-bethel, because there God had revealed himself to him when he fled from his brother(Genesis 35, 7)."

EL-ELOHE-ISRAEL (The God of Israel)

"And Jacob came safely to the city of Shechem, which is in the land of Canaan, on his way from Paddan-aram; and he camped before the city. And from the sons of Hamor, Shechem's father, he bought for a hundred pieces of money the piece of land on which he had pitched his tent. There he erected an altar and called it El-Elohe-Israel* (Genesis 33,18-20)." * "God, the God of Israel"

ELI ("My God")

"Now from the sixth hour there was darkness over all the land until the ninth hour. And about the ninth hour Jesus cried with a loud voice, 'Eli, Eli, lama sabachthani?' that is, 'My God, my God, why hast thou forsaken me (Matthew 27, 45-46)?' "

ELOI (another term for "My God")

"And when the sixth hour had come, there was darkness over the whole land until the ninth hour. And at the ninth hour Jesus cried with a loud voice, 'Eloi, Eloi, lama sabachthani?' which means, 'My God, my God, why hast thou forsaken me (Mark 15, 33-34)?' "

ELROI ("A God who Sees")

Hagar, fleeing into the wilderness, was found by "the angel of the LORD," believed by some to be the pre-incarnate Jesus, and told she would bear a son named Ishmael. "So she called the name of the LORD who spoke to her, 'Thou art a God of seeing;' for she said, 'Have I really seen God and remained alive after seeing him (Genesis 16,13)?' "
"Elroi" is the Hebrew for "Thou art a God of seeing."

EVERLASTING GOD

"Abraham planted a tamarisk tree in Beer-sheeba, and called there on the name of the LORD, the Everlasting God (Genesis 21, 33)."

"thy throne is established from of old;
thou art from everlasting (Psalm 93, 2)."

FAITHFUL AND TRUE

This term is primarily an attribute, or a description of God's character, although in the book of the Revelation, it is used as an actual name.

"God is faithful, by whom you were called into the fellowship of his Son, Jesus Christ our Lord (1 Corinthians 1, 9)."

"... God is faithful, and he will not let you be tempted beyond your strength, but with the temptation will also provide the way of escape, that you may be able to endure it (1 Corinthians 10, 13b)."

"May the God of peace himself sanctify you wholly; and may your spirit and soul and body be kept sound and blameless at the coming of our Lord Jesus Christ. He who calls you is faithful and he will do it (1 Thessalonians 5, 23-24)."

Jesus "... had to be made like his brethren in every respect, so that he might become a merciful and faithful high priest in the service of God, to make expiation for the sins of the people. For because he himself has suffered and been tempted, he is able to help those who are tempted (Hebrews 2, 17-18)."

"Therefore, brothers and sisters, holy partners in a heavenly calling, consider that Jesus, the apostle and high priest of our confession, was faithful to the one who appointed him, just as Moses also 'was faithful in all God's house.' Yet Jesus is worthy of more glory than Moses, just as the builder of a house has more honor than the house itself. (For every house is built by someone, but the builder of all things is God). Now Moses was faithful in all God's house as a servant, to testify to the things that would be spoken later. Christ, however, was faithful over God's house as a son, and we are his house if we hold firm the confidence and the pride that belong to hope (Hebrews 3,1-6 NRSV)."

"Let us hold fast the confession of our hope without wavering, for he who promised is faithful ... (Hebrews10, 23a)."

"By faith Sarah herself received power to conceive, even when she was past the age, since she considered him faithful who had promised (Hebrews 11,11)."

"... let those who suffer according to God's will do right and entrust their souls to a faithful Creator (1 Peter 4,19)."

"If we confess our sins, he is faithful and just and will forgive our sins and cleanse us from all unrighteousness (1 John 1, 9)."

"... Jesus Christ the faithful witness, the firstborn of the dead, and the ruler of the kings on earth (Revelation 1, 5)."

Jesus "... the faithful and true witness, the beginning of God's creation (Revelation 3, 14)."

"Then I saw heaven opened, and behold, a white horse! He who sat upon it is called Faithful and True, and in righteousness he judges and makes war (Revelation 19, 11)."

FATHER

"Father of the fatherless
          and protector of widows
is God in his holy habitation (Psalm 68, 5)."

"As a father pities his children,
   so the LORD pities those who fear him.
For he knows our frame;
   he remembers that we are dust (Psalm 103, 13-14)."

"For to us a child is born,
   to us a son is given;
and the government will be upon his shoulder,
   and his name will be called

      'Wonderful Counselor,

          Mighty God,

              Everlasting Father,

                    Prince of Peace (Isaiah 9, 6).' "

> "For you are our father,
> though Abraham does not know
>   us
> and Israel does not acknowledge
>   us;
> you, O LORD, are our father;
>   our Redeemer from of old is
>   your name (Isaiah 63, 16 NRSV)."

> "Yet, O LORD, you are our Father;
> we are the clay, and you are our
>   potter;
> we are all the work of your
>   hand (Isaiah 64, 8 NRSV)."

"... I thought you would call me, My Father, and would not turn from following me (Jeremiah 3, 19c)."

"... I am a father to Israel,
    and Ephraim is my first-born (Jeremiah 31, 9c)."

"If then I am a father, where is my honor? (Malachi 1, 6b)?"

We turn now to study a few New Testament references to God as Father. References in the Hebrew scriptures (Old Testament) were relatively rare.

The synoptic gospels (Matthew, Mark, and Luke) all have references to the baptism of Jesus. Jesus is called "my beloved Son" by God the Father. The first New Testament reference to God as our Father is:

"... let your light shine before others, so that they may see your good works and give glory to your Father in heaven
(Matthew 5, 16 NRSV)."

The Greek word used for "father" is "pater." In Mark's account of Jesus' agony in the Garden of Gethsemene, he combines the "abba" of "daddy" form of "father" with "pater."

" '... your Father knows what you need before you ask him. 'Pray then in this way: Our Father in heaven, hallowed be your name. Your kingdom come. Your will be done, on earth as it is in heaven. Give us this day our daily bread. And forgive us our debts, as we have also forgiven our debtors. And do not bring us to the time of trial, but rescue us from the evil one (Matthew 6, 8-13 NRSV).' "

It is very important to note the next two verses. " 'For if you forgive others their trespasses, your heavenly Father will also forgive you; but if you do not forgive others, neither will your Father forgive your trespasses (Matthew 6, 14-15 NRSV)."

"If you then, who are evil, know how to give good gifts to your children, how much more will your Father in heaven give good things to those who ask Him (Matthew 7, 11 NRSV)?"

"Not everyone who says to me, 'Lord, Lord,' will enter the kingdom of heaven, but only the one who does the will of my Father in heaven (Matthew 7, 21 NRSV)."

"Are not two sparrows sold for a penny? Yet not one of them will fall to the ground apart from your Father. And even the hairs of your head are all counted. So do not be afraid; you are of more value than any sparrows.

Everyone therefore who acknowledges me before others, I also will acknowledge before your Father in heaven; but whoever denies me before others, I also will deny before my Father in heaven (Matthew 10, 29-33 NRSV)."

"... whoever does the will of my Father in heaven is my brother, and sister, and mother (Matthew 12, 50)."

"Whenever you stand praying, forgive, if you have anything against anyone; so that your Father in heaven may also forgive you your trespasses (Mark 11, 25 NRSV)."

In the Garden of Gethsemane, Jesus prayed, " 'Abba, Father for you all things are possible; remove this cup from me; yet, not what I want, but what you want (Mark 14, 36 NRSV).' "

Jesus tells us, "Be merciful, even as your Father is merciful (Luke 6, 36)."

"And do not seek what you are to eat and what you are to drink, nor be of anxious mind. For all the nations of the world seek these things; and your Father knows that you need them. Instead, seek his kingdom and these things shall be yours as well.

Fear not, little flock, for it is your Father's good pleasure to give you the kingdom (Luke 12, 29-32)."

Probably the best known example of how God loves us as Father is found in Jesus' parable of the Prodigal Son:

"There was a man who had two sons; and the younger of them said to his father, 'Father, give me the share of property that falls to me.' And he divided his living between them. Not many days later, the younger son gathered all he had and took his journey into a far country and there he squandered his property in loose living. And when he had spent everything, a great famine arose in that country, and he began to be in want. So he went and joined himself to one of the citizens of that country, who sent him into his fields to feed swine. And he would gladly have fed on the pods that the swine ate; and no one gave him anything. But when he came to himself he said, 'How many of my father's hired servants have bread enough and to spare, but I perish here with hunger! I will arise and go to my father, and I will say to him, 'Father, I have sinned against heaven and before you; I am no longer worthy to be called your son; treat me as one of your hired servants.' And he arose and came to his father. But while he was yet a distance, his father saw him and had compassion, and ran and embraced him and kissed him. And the son said to him, 'Father, I have sinned against heaven and before you; I am no longer worthy to be called your son.' But the father said to his servants, 'Bring quickly the best robe and put it on him; and put a ring on his hand, and shoes on his feet; and bring the fatted calf and kill it, and let us eat and make merry; for this my son was dead, and is alive again; he was lost, and is found.' And they began to make merry. Now his elder son was in the field; and as he came and drew near the house, he heard music and dancing. And he called one of the servants and asked what this meant. And he said to him, 'Your brother has come, and your father has killed to fatted calf, because he has received him safe and sound.' But he was angry and refused to go in. His father came out and entreated him, but he answered his father, 'Lo, these many years I have served you, and I never disobeyed your command; yet you never gave me a kid, that I might make merry with my friends. But when this son of yours came, who has devoured your living with harlots, you killed for him the fatted calf!' And he said to him, 'Son, you are always with me, and all that is mine is yours. It was fitting to make merry and glad, for this your brother was dead, amd is alive; he was lost, and is found (Luke 15, 11-32).' "

As Thielicke says, in THE WAITING FATHER,
"The prodigal son -- this is I, this is you! And the
father -- this is our Father in heaven who is waiting for us."

                      Helmut Thielcke
                      THE WAITING FATHER, p. 18
                      Harper and Row Publishers 1959

On the cross "... Jesus, crying with a loud voice, said, 'Father, into thy hands I commit my spirit (Luke 23, 46a)!' "

Before His ascension, Jesus said, "And behold, I send the promise of my Father upon you; but stay in the city until you are clothed with power from on high (Luke 24, 49)."

"And the Word became flesh and dwelt among us, full of grace and truth; we have beheld his glory, glory as of the only Son of the Father. (John bore witness to him, and cried, 'This was he of whom I said, 'He who comes after me ranks before me, for he was before me.') And from his fulness have we all received, grace upon grace. For the law was given through Moses; grace and truth came through Jesus Christ. No one has ever seen God; the only Son, who is in the bosom of the Father, he has made him known (John 1, 14-18)."

"... the hour is coming, and now is, when the true worshippers will worship the Father in spirit and truth, for such the Father seeks to worship him. God is spirit and those who worship him in spirit and truth (John 4, 23-24)."

"Jesus said... 'Truly, truly, I say to you, the Son can do nothing of his own accord, but only what he sees the Father doing; for whatever he does, that the Son does likewise (John 5, 19)."

"The Father judges no one but has given all judgment to the Son, so that all may honor the Son just as they honor the Father. Anyone who does not honor the Son does not honor the Father who sent him (John 5, 22-23 NRSV)."

"Everything that the Father gives me will come to me, and anyone who comes to me I will never drive away; for I have come down from heaven, not to do my own will, but the will of him who sent me. And this is the will of him who sent me, that I should lose nothing of all that he has given me, but raise it up on the last day. This is indeed the will of my Father, that all who see the Son and believe in him may have eternal life; and I will raise them up on the last day (John 6, 37-40 NRSV)."

Jesus said, "The Father and I are one (John 10, 30 NRSV)."

"Let not your hearts be troubled; believe in God, believe also in me. In my Father's house are many rooms; if it were not so, would I have told you that I go to prepare a place for you? And when I go and prepare a place for you, I will come again and will take you to myself, that where I am you may be also (John 14, 1-3)."

Philip said to Jesus, " 'Lord, show us the Father, and we will be satisfied.' Jesus said to him, 'Have I been with you all this time, Philip. and you still do not know me? Whoever has seen me has seen the Father. How can you say, 'Show us the Father'? Do you not believe that I am in the Father and the Father is in me? The words that I say to you I do not speak on my own; but the Father who dwells in me does his works. Believe me that I am in the Father and the Father is in me; but if you do not, then believe me because of the works themselves
(John 14, 8-11 NRSV)."

"... the Father himself loves you, because you have loved me and have believed that I came from the Father (John 16, 27)."

To Mary Magdalene, after his resurrection, Jesus said, "... I am ascending to my Father and your Father, to my God and your God (John 20, 17b)."

To his disciples, he said, " 'Peace be with you. As the Father has sent me, even so I send you (John 20, 21).' "

"And while staying with them he charged them not to depart from Jerusalem, but to wait for the promise of the Father, which, he said, 'you heard from me, for John baptized with water, but before many days you shall be baptized with the Holy Spirit.' So when they had come together, they asked him, 'Lord, will you at this time restore the kingdom to Israel?' He said to them, 'It is not for you to know times of seasons which the Father has fixed by his own authority. But you shall receive power when the Holy Spirit has come upon you; and you shall be my witnesses in Jerusalem and Samaria and to the ends of the earth
(Acts 1, 4-8).' "

"For all who are led by the Spirit of God are children of God. For you did not receive a spirit of slavery to fall back into fear, but you have received a spirit of adoption. When we cry, 'Abba! Father!' it is that very Spirit bearing witness with our spirit that we are children of God and joint heirs with Christ -- if, in fact, we suffer with him so that we may also be glorified with him (Romans 8, 14-16 NRSV)."

"... for us there is one God, the Father, from whom are all things and for whom we exist, and one Lord, Jesus Christ, through whom are all things and through whom we exist (1 Corinthians 8, 6)."

"Blessed be the God and Father of our Lord Jesus Christ, the Father of mercies and God of all comfort, who comforts us in all our affliction, so that we may be able to comfort those who are in any affliction, with the comfort with which we ourselves are comforted by God (2 Corinthians 1, 3,4)."

"... I will be a father to you,
and you shall be my sons and daughters,
says the Lord Almighty (2 Corinthians 6,18)."

"And because you are children, God has sent the Spirit of his Son into our hearts, crying, 'Abba! Father!' So you are no longer a slave but a child, and if a child then also an heir, through God (Galatians 4, 6 NRSV)."

"Blessed be the God and Father of our Lord Jesus Christ, who has blessed us in Christ with every spiritual blessing in the heavenly places, even as he chose us in him before the foundation of the world, that we should be holy and blameless before him (Ephesians 1, 3,4)."

"I do not cease to give thanks for you, remembering you in my prayers, that the God of our Lord Jesus Christ, the Father of glory, may give you a spirit of wisdom and of revelation in the knowledge of him (Ephesians 1, 16.17)."

"There is one body and one Spirit, just as you were called to the one hope that belongs to your call, one Lord, one faith, one baptism, one God and Father of us all, who is above all and through all and in all (Ephesians 4, 4-6)."

"Always and for everything giving thanks in the name of our Lord Jesus Christ to God the Father (Ephesians 5, 20)."

"To our God and Father be glory for ever and ever. Amen (Philippians 4, 20)."

"And whatever you do, in word or deed, do everything in the name of the Lord Jesus, giving thanks to God the Father through him (Colossians 3, 17)."

"Endure trials for the sake of discipline. God is treating you as children; for what child is there whom a parent does not discipline? Moreover, we had human parents to discipline us, and we respected them. Should we not be even more willing to be subject to the Father of spirits and live (Hebrews 12, 7, 9-10 NRSV)?"

"Every good endowment and every perfect gift is from above, coming down from the Father of lights with whom there is no variation or shadow due to change. Of his own will he brought us forth by the word of truth that we should be a kind of first fruits of his creatures (James 1,17-18)."

"Blessed be the God and Father of our Lord Jesus Christ! By his great mercy we have been born anew to a living hope through the resurrection of Jesus Christ from the dead, and to an inheritance which is imperishable, undefiled, and unfading, kept in heaven for you (1 Peter 1, 3,4)."

"... our fellowship is with the Father and with his Son Jesus Christ (1 John 1, 3b)."

"My little children, I am writing these things to you so that you may not sin. But if anyone does sin, we have an advocate with the Father, Jesus Christ the righteous; and he is the atoning sacrifice for our sins, and not for ours only but also for the sins of the whole world.

Now by this we may be sure that we know him, if we obey his commandments (1 John 2, 1-3 NRSV)."

"No one who denies the Son has the Father; everyone who confesses the Son has the Father also. (1 John 2, 23 NRSV)."

"See what love the Father has given us, that we should be called children of God; and so we are (1 John 3, 1a)."

Jesus says "I reprove and discipline those whom I love. Be earnest, therefore, and repent. Listen! I am standing at the door, knocking; if you hear my voice and open the door, I will come in to you and eat with you, and you with me. To the one who conquers I will give a place with me on my throne, just as I myself conquered and sat down with my Father on his throne (Revelation 3, 19-21 NRSV)."

THE FIRST AND THE LAST

" When I saw him, I fell at his feet as though dead. But he placed his right hand on me, saying, 'Do not be afraid; I am the first and the last, and the living one. I was dead, and see, I am alive forever and ever; and I have the keys of Death and of Hades (Revelation 1, 17-18 NRSV)."

FORERUNNER

"We have this as a sure and steadfast anchor of the soul, a hope that enters into the inner shrine behind the curtain, where Jesus has gone as a forerunner on our behalf, having become a high priest for ever after the order of Melchizedek (Hebrews 6, 19, 20)."

FORTRESS

"And David spoke to the LORD the words of this song on the day when the LORD delivered him from the hand of all his enemies, and from the hand of Saul. He said,

'The LORD is my rock, and my fortress, and my deliverer...' "
(2 Samuel 22, 1-2)."

"You who live in the shelter of the Most High, who abide in the shadow of the Almighty, will say to the LORD, 'My refuge and my fortress; my God, in whom I trust (Psalm 91, 1-2 NRSV).' "

FRIEND

"Thus the LORD used to speak to Moses face to face, as one speaks to a friend (Exodus 33, 11a NRSV)."

"Did you not, O our God, drive out the inhabitants of this land before your people Israel, and give it forever to the descendants of your friend Abraham (2 Chronicles 20, 7 NRSV)?"

"... the Son of man... a friend of tax-collectors and sinners (Matthew 11, 19, Luke 7, 34)."

When Judas came to betray Jesus with a kiss, Jesus said to him, "Friend, why are you here (Matthew 26, 50)?"

" 'I tell you, my friends, do not fear those who kill the body, and after that have no more they can do. But I will warn you whom to fear: fear him who, after he has killed, has power to cast into hell; yes, I tell you, fear him! Are not five sparrows sold for two pennies? And not one of them is forgotten before God. Why, even the hairs of your head are all numbered. Fear not; you are of more value than many sparrows (Luke 12, 4-7)."

" 'Our friend Lazarus has fallen asleep, but I go to awaken him out of sleep (John 11, 11)"

Because Jesus loved Martha and her sister and Lazarus , He allowed their temporary suffering, which was far outweighed by their increased revelation of who Jesus, their friend, really was. After Jesus' declaration to Martha -- 'I am the resurrection and the life; he who believes in me, though he die, yet shall he live, and whoever lives and believes in me shall never die. Do you believe this?' (vv. 25-26) -- she responds, " 'Yes, Lord; I believe that you are the Christ, the Son of God, he who is coming into the world (v. 27).' " In the next chapter, we see Mary anointing the feet of Jesus.

Jesus said, " 'This is my commandment, that you love one another as I have loved you. No one has greater love than this, to lay down one's life for one's friends. You are my friends if you do what I command you. I do not call you servants any longer, because the servant does not know what the master is doing; but I have called you friends, because I have made known to you everything that I have heard from my Father. You did not choose me but I chose you ((John 15, 12-16a NRSV).' "

"Was not Abraham our father justified by works, when he offered his son Isaac upon the altar? You see that faith was active along with his works, and faith was completed by works, and the scripture was fulfilled which says, 'Abraham believed God, and it was reckoned to him as righteousness'; and he was called the friend of God (James 2, 21-23)."

GATE

"... Jesus said to them, 'Very truly I tell you, I am the gate for the sheep. All who come before me are thieves and bandits; but the sheep did not listen to them. I am the gate. Whoever enters by me will be saved, and you will come in and out and find pasture. The thief comes only to steal and kill and destroy. I came that they may have life, and have it abundantly (John 10, 7-10 NRSV).' "

GOD

"In the beginning God...." (Genesis 1, 1)

The Hebrew word for "God" in this verse is " 'elohiym.' " The word "YeHOVAH" is another Hebrew word for God.

"When Abram was ninety-nine years old the LORD appeared to Abram, and said to him, 'I am God Almighty; walk before me, and be blameless. And I will make my covenant between me and you, and will multiply you exceedingly (Genesis 17, 1-2).' "
The word for "God" here is "El Shaddai."

Jacob "... erected an altar and called it El-Elohe-Israel (Genesis 33, 20)." "El Elohe" means "God, the God of Israel."

"And Jacob came to Luz (that is, Bethel), which is in the land of Canaan, he and all the people who were with him, and there he built an altar, and called the place El-bethel, because there God had revealed himself to him when he fled from his brother (Genesis 35, 6-7)."
El-bethel means "house of God."

Earlier in his life, after a powerfully prophetic dream, "... Jacob awoke from his sleep and said, 'Surely the LORD is in this place; and I did not know it. How awesome is this place! This is none other than the house of God, and this is the gate of heaven (Genesis 28, 16,17).' "

"The LORD of hosts is with us; the God of Jacob is our refuge (Psalm 46, 7,11)."

"... the LORD, whose name is the God of hosts (Amos 5, 27)."

" 'Behold, a virgin shall conceive and bear a son,
and his name shall be called
Emmanuel'
(which means, God with us) (Matthew 1, 23)."
(quotation from prophecy in Isaiah 7, 14)

"In the beginning was the Word, and the Word was with God, and the Word was God (John 1, 1)."

The term "Word" is, of course, a reference to Jesus.

HEAD

Jesus is "... head over all things for the church, which is his body (Ephesians 1, 22)."

"... speaking the truth in love, we are to grow up in every way into him who is the head, into Christ... (Ephesians 4, 15)."

Mutual respect! "Be subject to one another out of reverence for Christ. Wives, be subject to your husbands, as to the Lord. For the husband is the head of the wife as Christ is head of the body, and is himself its Savior. As the church is subject to Christ, so let wives also be subject in everything to their husbands. Husbands, love your wives, as Christ loved the church and gave himself for her ... (Ephesians 5, 21-25)."

Jesus "... is the head of the body, the church; he is the beginning, the firstborn from the dead, so that he might come to have first place in everything. For in him all the fullness of God was pleased to dwell, and through him God was pleased to reconcile to himself all things, whether on earth or in heaven, by making peace through the blood of his cross (Colossians 1,18-20 NRSV)."

Jesus, "... the head, from whom the whole body, nourished and held together by its ligaments and sinews, grows with a growth that is from God (Colossians 2, 19 NRSV)."

"... the head of every man is Christ, the head of a woman is her husband, and the head of Christ is God (1 Corinthians 11, 3)."

"To you therefore who believe, he is precious,
> but for those who do not believe,

'The very stone which the builders rejected
> has become the head of the corner...(1 Peter 2, 7).' "

HEALER

The references in the Hebrew Scriptures (Old Testament) to the word "heal" are translations of the Hebrew word "raphah." This word means to heal or to mend by stitching. It can also mean to repair and to make whole in a total, thorough sense. Notice that it is not a matter of waving a magic wand, and, "Abracadabra, you are healed."

No. It takes time; either a short time or sometimes a very long time, to "stitch" us back together. We can take comfort in the fact that it is God who is doing the mending and the stitching. When the healing process is finished, we shall indeed be whole.

"If you will diligently hearken to the voice of the LORD your God, and do that which is right in his eyes, and give heed to his commandments and keep all his statutes, I will put none of the diseases upon you which I put upon the Egyptians; for I am the LORD your healer (Exodus 15, 26)."

"Bless the LORD, O my soul,
   and forget not all his benefits,
who forgives all you iniquity,
   who heals all your diseases ... (Psalm 103, 3)."

"... they cried to the LORD in their trouble,
   and he delivered them from their distress;
he sent forth his word, and healed them,
   and delivered them from destruction (Psalm 107, 19b-20)."

"He heals the brokenhearted,
   and binds up their wounds (Psalm 147, 3)."

"I have seen his ways, but I will heal him ... (Isaiah 57, 18a)."

"Return, O faithless children,
   I will heal your faithlessness (Jeremiah 3, 22a NRSV)."

"Heal me, O LORD, and I shall be healed; save me, and I shall be saved; for you are my praise (Jeremiah 17, 14 NRSV)."

"... I will restore health to you,
   and your wounds I will heal,
     says the LORD (Jeremiah 30, 17a)."

" 'Come, let us return to the LORD;
for he has torn, that he may heal us;
he has stricken, and he will bind us up (Hosea 6, 1)' "

"I will heal their faithlessness ... (Hosea 14, 4a)."

"... for you who fear my name the sun of righteousness shall rise, with healing in its wings. You shall go forth leaping like calves from the stall (Malachi 4, 2)."

In the following passages from the New Testament, we see Jesus continuing the work of healing. He shows, by his desire and ability to heal, that it is God's will that we be made whole.

Jesus "... went about all Galilee, teaching in their synagogues and preaching the gospel of the kingdom and healing every disease and every infirmity among the people (Matthew 4,23)."

"As he entered Capernaum, a centurion came forward to him, beseeching him and saying, 'Lord, my servant is lying paralyzed at home, in terrible distress.' And he said to him, 'I will come and heal him.' But the centurion answered him, 'Lord, I am not worthy to have you come under my roof; but only say the word, and my servant will be healed.

And to the centurion Jesus said, 'Go; be it done for you as you have believed.' And the servant was healed at that very moment (Matthew 8, 5-8,13)."

"And Jesus went about all the cities and villages, teaching in their synagogues and preaching the gospel of the kingdom, and healing every disease and every infirmity (Matthew 9, 35)."

"And many followed him, and he healed them all
(Matthew 12, 15b)."

"And he came to Nazareth, where he had been brought up; and he went to the synagogue, as his custom was, on the sabbath day. And he stood up to read; and there was given to him the book of the prophet Isaiah. He opened the book and found the place where it is written,

'The Spirit of the Lord is upon me,
because he has anointed me to preach good news to the poor.
He has sent me to proclaim release to the captives
and recovery of sight to the blind,
to set at liberty those who are oppressed,
to proclaim the acceptable year of the Lord.'

And he closed the book, and gave it back to the attendant, and sat down; and the eyes of all in the synagogue were fixed on him. And he began to say to them, 'Today this scripture has been fulfilled in your hearing (Luke 4, 16-21).'"

"... the power of the Lord was with him to heal (Luke 5, 17b)."

"When he was abused, he did not return abuse; when he suffered, he did not threaten; but he entrusted himself to the one who judges justly. He himself bore our sins on the cross, so that, free from sins, we might live for righteousness; by his wounds you have been healed. For you were going astray like sheep, but now you have returned to the shepherd and guardian of your souls (1 Peter 2, 23-25 NRSV)."

HELPER

"... God helped the Levites who were carrying the ark of the covenant of the Lord (1 Chronicles 15, 26)."

"And when the captains of the chariots saw Jehoshsphat, they said, 'It is the king of Israel.' So they turned to fight against him; and Jehoshaphat cried out, and the Lord helped him. God drew them away from him ... (2 Chronicles 18, 31)."

"But you do see! Indeed you note trouble and grief, that you may take it into your hands; the helpless commit themselves to you; you have been the helper of the orphan (Psalm 10, 14 NRSV)."

"Hear, O LORD, and be gracious to me!
O LORD, be thou my helper (Psalm 30, 10)!"

"Behold, God is my helper;
the LORD is the upholder of my life (Psalm 54, 4)."

"And some of the men of Benjamin and Judah came to... David. Then the Spirit came upon Amasai ... and he said,

'We are yours, O David;
and with you, O son of Jesse!
Peace, peace to you,
and peace to your helpers!
For your God helps you (1 Chronicles 12, 16, 18)."

Speaking of the promised Holy Spirit, Jesus tells his disciples, "And I will ask the Father, and he will give you another Advocate, to be with you forever. This is the Spirit of truth whom the world cannot receive, because it neither sees him nor knows him. You know him, because he abides with you, and he will be in you. I have said these things to you while I am still with you. But the Advocate, the Holy Spirit, whom the Father will send in my name, will teach you everything, and will remind you of all that I have said to you. When the Advocate comes, whom I will send to you from the Father, the Spirit of truth who comes from the Father, he will testify on my behalf (John 14, 16-17, 15, 26 NRSV)."

The New American Standard Bible uses the name "Helper." The New Jerusalem Bible uses the name "Paraclete." The King James Version uses the name "Comforter." The beautiful Knox version of The Holy Bible speaks of the Holy Spirit who is coming to befriend us (John 14, 16; John 15, 26).

"Likewise the Spirit helps us in our weakness; for we do not know how to pray as we ought, but that very Spirit intercedes with sighs too deep for words. And God, who searches the heart, knows what is the mind of the Spirit, because the Spirit intercedes for the saints according to the will of God (Romans 8, 26-27 NRSV)."

"... The LORD is my helper,
I will not be afraid .. .(Hebrews 13, 6)."

HOLY (includes references to the Holy Spirit)

The following verses refer to the holiness surrounding God.

"Look down from heaven and see,
from thy holy and glorious habitation (Isaiah 63, 15)."

"God is king over the nations; God sits on his holy throne (Psalm 47, 8 NRSV)."

"Great is the LORD and greatly to be praised
    in the city of our God!
His holy mountain, beautiful in elevation,
    is the joy of all the earth,
    Mount Zion, in the far north,
    the city of the great King (Psalm 48, 1-2)."

The next verses refer to the holiness of God's people.

Exodus 28 describes the priestly vestments.

"You shall make a rosette of pure gold, and engrave on it, like the engraving of a signet, 'Holy to the LORD.' You shall fasten it on the turban with a blue cord; it shall be on Aaron's forehead ... (Exodus 28, 36-38a NRSV)."

"Ascribe to the LORD the glory of his name;
worship the LORD in holy array (Psalm 29, 2)."

"Consecrate yourselves ... and be holy; for I am the LORD your God. Keep my statutes, and do them; I am the LORD who sanctify you (Leviticus 20, 7-8)."

God "... disciplines us for our good, that we may share his holiness. For the moment all discipline seems painful rather than pleasant; later it yields the peaceful fruit of righteousness to those who have been trained by it (Hebrews 12, 10b-11)."

"Blessed be the Lord God of Israel, for he has looked favorably on his people and redeemed them. He has raised up a mighty savior for us in the house of his servant, David, as he spoke through the mouth of his holy prophets from of old, so that we would be saved from our enemies and from the hand of all who hate us. Thus he has shown the mercy promised to our ancestors, and has remembered his holy covenant, the oath that he sword to our ancestor Abraham, to grant us that we, being rescued from the hands of our enemies, might server him without fear, in holiness and righteousness before him all our days. And you, child, will be called the prophet of the Most High; for you will go before the Lord to prepare his ways, to give knowledge of salvation to his people for the forgiveness of their sins. By the tender mercy of our God, the dawn from on high will break upon us, to give light to those who sit in darkness and in the shadow of death, to guide our feet into the way of peace (Luke 1, 68-79, NRSV)."

This is the first part of the poem or canticle known as the Benedictus. It is ascribed to Zechariah, father of John the Baptist. Zechariah spoke these words after the birth of his son.

" 'Who is like you, O LORD, among
    the gods?
Who is like you, majestic in
    holiness,
awesome in splendor, doing
    wonders (Exodus 15, 11 NRSV)?"

".. a holy God ... a jealous God ... (Joshua 24, 19)."

" 'There is none holy like the LORD,
there is none besides thee;
   there is no rock like our God (1Samuel 2, 2).' "

" 'Who is able to stand before the LORD, this holy God
                    (1 Samuel 6, 20a)?"

"Glory in his holy name;
   let the hearts of those who seek the LORD rejoice
                    (1 Chronicles 16, 10)!"

"... thou art holy,
enthroned on the praises of Israel (Psalm 22, 3)."

"Our soul waits for the LORD;
he is our help and shield.
... our heart is glad in him,
because we trust in his holy name (Psalm 33, 20-21)."

"Create in me a clean heart, O God,
and put a new and right spirit within me.
Cast me not away from thy presence,
and take not thy holy Spirit from me (Psalm 51, 10-11)."

"Thy way, O God, is holy.
What God is great like our God?
Thou art the LORD who workest wonders,
who hast manifested thy might among the peoples
                        (Psalm 77, 13-14)."

First of all, we recognize God's holiness. Then we see God in operation as a wonder-worker. If we reverse the order, we will have a distorted view and see God only as a wonder-worker. It is essential to reckon first with the fact that God is HOLY.

"My mouth will speak the praise of the LORD,
and let all flesh bless his holy name for ever and ever
                        (Psalm 145, 21)."

"But the LORD of hosts is exalted in justice,
and the Holy One shows himself holy in righteousness
                        (Isaiah 5, 16)."

"In the year that King Uzziah died I saw the LORD sitting upon a throne, high and lifted up; and his train filled the temple. Above him stood the seraphim; each had six wings; with two he covered his face, and with two he covered his feet, and with two he flew. And one called to another and said:

'Holy, holy, holy is the LORD of hosts;
the whole earth is full of his glory (Isaiah 6, 1-3).' "

"The light of Israel will become a fire,
and his Holy One a flame;
and it will burn and devour
his thorns and briers in one day (Isaiah 10, 17)."

"Shout for joy, O inhabitant of Zion,
for great in your midst is the Holy One of Israel (Isaiah 12, 6)."

In describing Zion restored, the writer says,

> "A highway shall be there,
> and it shall be called the Holy Way;
> the unclean shall not travel on it,
> but it shall be for God's people;
> no traveler, not even fools, shall go astray
> (Isaiah 35, 8 NRSV)."

"I am the LORD, your Holy One,
the Creator of Israel, your King (Isaiah 43, 15)."

"For your maker is your husband,
the LORD of hosts is his name;
and the Holy One of Israel is your Redeemer,
the God of the whole earth he is called (Isaiah 54, 5)."

> "For thus says the high and lofty one
>   who inhabits eternity,
>   whose name is Holy:
> I dwell in the high and holy place,
>   and also with those who are
>   contrite and humble in spirit,
>   to revive the spirit of the humble,
>   and to revive the heart of the contrite
> (Isaiah 57, 15 NRSV)."

"And my holy name I will make known in the midst of my people Israel; and I will not let my holy name be profaned any more; and the nations shall know that I am the LORD, the Holy One in Israel (Ezekiel 39, 7)."

Transition!

Guess Who is coming!

"Now the birth of Jesus Christ took place in this way. When his mother Mary had been betrothed to Joseph, before they came together she was found to be with child of the Holy Spirit (Matthew 1, 18)."

The understandably concerned Joseph was told "... do not fear to take Mary your wife, for that which is conceived in her is of the Holy Spirit; she will bear a son and you shall call his name Jesus, for he will save his people from their sins (Matthew 1, 20b, 21)."

John the Baptist announced " 'I baptize you with water for

repentance, but he who is coming after me is mightier than I, whose sandals I am not worthy to carry; he will baptize you with the Holy Spirit and with fire (Matthew 3, 11).' "

"Now the eleven disciples went to Galilee, to the mountain to which Jesus had directed them. And when they saw him they worshipped him; but some doubted. And Jesus came and said to them, 'All authority in heaven and on earth has been given to me. Go therefore and make disciples of all nations, baptizing them in the name of the Father and of the Son and of the Holy Spirit, teaching them to observe all that I have commanded you; and lo, I am with you always, to the close of the age (Matthew 28, 16-20).' "

"And they went into Capernaum; and immediately on the Sabbath he entered the synagogue and taught. And they were astonished at his teaching, for he taught them as one who had authority, and not as the scribes. And immediately there was in their synagogue a man with an unclean spirit; and he cried out, 'What have you to do with us, Jesus of Nazareth? Have you come to destroy us? I know who you are, the Holy One of God.' But Jesus rebuked him, saying, 'Be silent, and come out of him!' And the unclean spirit, convulsing him and crying with a loud voice, came out of him (Mark 1, 21-26)."

It is interesting to note that the evil spirits knew exactly who Jesus was!

" 'Truly, I say to you, all sins will be forgiven the sons of men, and whatever blasphemies they utter; but whoever blasphemes against the Holy Spirit never has forgiveness, but is guilty of an eternal sin'-- for they had said, 'He has an unclean spirit (Mark 3, 28-30).' "

"And when they bring you to trial and deliver you up, do not be anxious beforehand what you are to say; but say whatever is given you in that hour, for it is not you who speak, but the Holy Spirit (Mark 13, 11)."

John the Baptist "... will be filled with the Holy Spirit even from his mother's womb (Luke 1, 15b)."

The idea of being chosen for a special ministry since before birth is not new. The LORD said to Jeremiah, " 'Before I formed you in the womb I knew you, and before you were born I consecrated you; I appointed you a prophet to the nations (Jeremiah 1, 5).' "

At the Annunciation, the angel Gabriel said to Mary,

" 'The Holy Spirit will come upon you,
    and the power of the Most High will overshadow you;
  therefore the child to be born
  will be called holy,
    the Son of God (Luke 1, 35).' "

The Holy Spirit is the only explanation for the birth of Jesus and the only explanation for our new birth. Jesus said, " 'Truly, truly, I say to you, unless one is born of water and the Spirit, he cannot enter the kingdom of God. That which is born of the flesh is flesh, and that which is born of the Spirit is spirit. Do not marvel that I said to you, 'You must be born anew* (John 3, 5-8).' "   * or "from above"

"... when Jesus also had been baptized and was praying, the heaven was opened, and the Holy Spirit descended upon him in bodily form, as a dove, and a voice came from heaven, 'Thou art my beloved Son; with thee I am well pleased (Luke 3, 21b-22).' "

"And Jesus, full of the Holy Spirit, returned from the Jordan, and was led by the Spirit for forty days in the wilderness, tempted by the devil." After the temptations, which he overcame by quoting Scripture, "... Jesus returned in the power of the Spirit into Galilee ... (Luke 4, 1,2a,14a).' "

"And he went down to Capernaum, a city of Galilee. And he was teaching them on the sabbath; and they were astonished at his teaching, for his word was with authority. And in the synagogue there was a man who had the spirit of an unclean demon; and he cried out with a loud voice, 'Ah! What have you to do with us, Jesus of Nazareth? Have you come to destroy us? I know who you are, the Holy One of God.' " (Luke 4, 31-34)

In his teaching on prayer, Jesus said, "... Ask, and it will be given you; seek, and you will find; knock, and it will be opened to you. For every one who asks receives, and he who seeks finds, and to him who knocks it will be opened. What father among you, if his son asks for a fish, will instead of a fish give him a serpent; or if he asks for an egg, will give him a scorpion? If you then, who are evil, know how to give good gifts to your children, how much more will the heavenly Father give the Holy Spirit to those who ask him (Luke 11, 9-13)!"

"On the last day of the feast, the great day, Jesus stood up and proclaimed, 'If any one thirst, let him come to me and drink. He who believes in me, as the scripture has said, 'Out of his heart shall flow rivers of living water.' Now this he said about the Spirit, which those who believed in him were to receive; for as yet the Spirit had not been given, because Jesus was not yet glorified (John 7, 37-39)."

In his farewell discourse to his followers, Jesus said, "the Counselor, the Holy Spirit, whom the Father will send in my name, he will teach you all things, and bring to your remembrance all that I have said to you (John 14, 25-26)."

In his high priestly prayer, Jesus says, "And now I am no longer in the world, but they are in the world, and I am coming to you. Holy Father, protect them in your name that you have given me, so that they may be one, as we are one (John 17, 11 NRSV)."

On the evening of the resurrection, Jesus came to the disciples and said, " 'Peace be with you.' When he had said this, he showed them his hands and his side. Then the disciples were glad when they saw the Lord. Jesus said to them again, 'Peace be with you. As the Father has sent me, even so I send you.' And when he had said this, he breathed on them, and said to them, 'Receive the Holy Spirit. If you forgive the sins of any, they are forgiven; if you retain the sins of any, they are retained (John 20, 19b-23).' "

"When the day of Pentecost had come, they were all together in one place. And suddenly from heaven there came a sound like the rush of a violent wind, and it filled the entire house where they were sitting. Divided tongues, as of fire, appeared among them, and a tongue rested on each of them. All of them were filled with the Holy Spirit and began to speak in other languages, as the Spirit gave them ability (Acts 2, 1-4 NRSV)."

Peter, explaining this manifestation of the Holy Spirit, said, "... this is what was spoken through the prophet Joel: 'In the last days it will be, God declares, that I will pour out my Spirit upon all flesh, and your sons and your daughters will prophesy, and your young men shall see visions, and your old men shall dream dreams, Even upon my slaves, both men and women, in those days I will pour out my Spirit, and they shall prophesy. And I will show portents in the heaven above and signs on the earth below, blood, and fire, and smoky mist. The sun shall be turned to darkness and the moon to blood, before the coming of the Lord's great and glorious day. Then everyone who calls on the name of the Lord shall be saved (Acts. 2, 16-21 NRSV)."

The book of Acts chronicles the mighty works of the Holy Spirit through the apostles -- that's why this book of the Bible is sometimes called the Acts of the Holy Spirit.

"I appeal to you therefore ... by the mercies of God, to present your bodies as a living sacrifice, holy and acceptable to God, which is your spiritual worship (Romans 12, 1)."

"For the kingdom of God is not food and drink but righteousness and peace and joy in the Holy Spirit ... (Romans 14, 17)."

"May the God of hope fill you with all joy and peace in believing, so that by the power of the Holy Spirit you may abound in hope (Romans 15, 13)."

"Do you not know that your body is a temple of the Holy Spirit within you, which you have from God? You are not your own; you were bought with a price. So glorify God in your body (1 Corinthians 6, 19-20)."

"Therefore I want you to understand that no one speaking by the Spirit of God ever says, 'Jesus be cursed!' and no one can say 'Jesus is Lord' except by the Holy Spirit (1 Corinthians 12, 3)."

"The grace of the Lord Jesus Christ and the love of God and the fellowship of the Holy Spirit be with you all (2 Corinthians 13, 14)."

"... as he who called you is holy, be holy yourselves in all your conduct; since it is written, 'You shall be holy, for I am holy (1 Peter 1, 15-16).'"

The Apocalypse allows us a glimpse a scene in heaven in which God is praised by four creatures who "... never cease to sing,

'Holy, holy, holy, is the Lord God Almighty,
 who was and is and is to come (Revelation 4, 8)!'"

HOPE OF ISRAEL

"O Hope of Israel, O LORD, its savior in time of trouble ... (Jeremiah 14, 8a NRSV)."

HUSBAND

"For your Maker is your husband,
 the LORD of hosts is his name...(Isaiah 54, 5)."

I AM

"But Moses said to God, 'If I come to the Israelites and say to them, 'The God of your ancestors has sent me to you,' and they ask me, 'What is his name?' what shall I say to them?' God said to Moses, 'I AM WHO I AM.' He said further, 'Thus you shall say to the Israelites, 'I AM has sent me to you.' God also said to Moses, 'Thus you shall say to the Israelites, 'The LORD, the God of your ancestors, the God of Abraham, the God of Isaac, and the God of Jacob, has sent me to you': This is my name forever, and this is my title for all generations. Go and assemble the elders of Israel, and say to them, 'The LORD, the God of your ancestors, the God of Abraham, of Isaac, and of Jacob, has appeared to me, saying: I have given heed to you and to what has been done to you in Egypt (Exodus 3, 13-16 NRSV).' "

Throughout his ministry, Jesus took His Father's statement of identity, "I AM" and translated, through his life, its meaning. He said,

> "I am the bread of life...." (John 6, 35a)
> "I am the living bread...." (John 6, 51a)
> "I am the light of the world...." (John 8, 12a)
> "I am the door of the sheep...." (John 10, 7b)
> "I am the good shepherd...." (John 10, 11a)
> "I am the true vine and my Father is the vinedresser (John 15, 1)."

These, and all Jesus' other "I am" statements are summed up in his ultimate statement of identity, "... 'before Abraham was, I am.' " (John 8, 58b)

JEALOUS

"... you shall worship no other god, for the LORD, whose name is Jealous, is a jealous God ...(Exodus 34, 14)."

"... the LORD your God is a devouring fire, a jealous God (Deuteronomy 4, 24)."

"You shall not go after other gods, of the gods of the peoples who are round about you; for the LORD your God in the midst of you is a jealous God ... (Deuteronomy 6, 15a)."

"... a holy God ... a jealous God .. .(Joshua 24, 19a)."

"... I will restore the fortunes of Jacob, and have mercy on the whole house of Israel; and I will be jealous for my holy name (Ezekiel 39, 25)."

" 'Thus says the LORD of hosts: I am jealous for Zion with great jealousy, and I am jealous for her with great wrath (Zechariah 8, 2)."

"The LORD is a jealous God ... (Nahum 1, 2a)."

"Shall we provoke the Lord to jealousy (1 Corinthians 10, 22)?"

JESUS

No matter how many times we hear the story of Jesus, we never cease to marvel at God's ways.

"Now the birth of Jesus the Messiah took place in this way. When his mother Mary had been engaged to Joseph, but before they lived together, she was found to be with child from the Holy Spirit. When her husband Joseph, being a righteous man and unwilling to expose her to public disgrace, planned to dismiss her quietly. But just as he had resolved to do this, an angel of the Lord appeared to him in a dream and said, 'Joseph, son of David, do not be afraid to take Mary as your wife into your home, for child conceived in he is from the Holy Spirit. She will bear a son, and you are to name him Jesus, for he will save his people from their sins. All this took place to fulfill what had been spoken by the Lord through the prophet;

'Look, the virgin shall conceive and bear a son,
and they shall name him Emmanuel,'

which means 'God is with us.' When Joseph awoke from sleep, he did as the angel of the Lord had commanded him; he took her as his wife, but had no marital relations with her until she had borne a son; and he named him Jesus (Matthew 1, 18-25 NRSV)."

"... the angel Gabriel was sent from God to a city of Galilee named Nazareth, to a virgin betrothed to a man whose name was Joseph, of the

house of David; and the virgin's name was Mary. And he came to her and said,
'Hail, O favored one, the Lord is with you!'

But she was greatly troubled at the saying, and considered in her mind what sort of greeting this might be. And the angel said to her,

> 'Do not be afraid, Mary,
> for you have found favor with God.
> And behold, you will conceive in your womb
> and bear a son,
> and you shall call his name Jesus (Luke 1, 26-31).'"

"... to you is born this day in the city of David a Savior, who is Christ the Lord.

And at the end of eight days, when he was circumcised, he was called Jesus, the name given by the angel before he was conceived in the womb (Luke 2, 11, 21)."

JUDGE

"Shall not the Judge of all the earth do right (Genesis 18, 25b KJV)?"

(The word "Judge" is "shaphat," which has the sense of vindicate, defend, pronounce sentence, carry out the sentence, avenge)

God is speaking to Moses: "Say therefore to the people of Israel, 'I am the LORD, and I will bring you out from under the burdens of the Egyptians, and I will deliver you from their bondage, and I will redeem you with an outstretched arm and with great acts of judgment (Exodus 6, 6).'"

"For the LORD shall judge his people …
            (Deuteronomy 32, 36a KJV)."

In the NRSV, this verse reads, "Indeed the LORD will vindicate his people, have compassion on his servants, when he sees that their power is gone, neither bond nor free remaining (Deuteronomy 32, 36 NRSV)."

This verse is another good reason to have at least one modern translation on hand. The word "judge" might convey a rather deeply oppressive meaning.

The word, "vindicate," on the other hand, is freeing for all involved. The Hebrew is "duwn," which views the judge as umpire or one who ministers judgment.

"The LORD will judge the ends of the earth …(1 Samuel 2, 10b).

(from the song of Hannah)
"Let the heavens be glad, and let the
 earth rejoice,
and let them say among the
 nations, 'The LORD reigns!'
Let the sea roar, and all that fills it,
 let the field exult, and everything
  in it!
Then shall the trees of the wood
 sing for joy
before the LORD, for he comes to
 judge the earth.
O give thanks to the LORD, for he
 is good;
for his steadfast love endures for
 ever!"
         1 Chronicles 16, 30-34
         (This passage also shows
         the ancient Israelite perception
         of joy coming from God's judgment).

Faced with a seemingly insurmountable obstacle, namely the fast approaching armies of the enemies, King Jehoshaphat prays to God,

" 'O our God, will you not execute judgment upon them? For we are powerless against this great multitude that is coming against us. We do not know what to do, but our eyes are on you (2 Chronicles 20, 12 NRSV).' " This, of course, is the famous passage in which God's people are told,

"Do not fear or be dismayed at this
great multitude; for the battle is
not yours but God's (2 Chronicles 20, 15b NRSV)."

The king appointed people to sing and
praise the LORD, and as they did so,
their enemies were routed.

"God is a righteous judge,
and a God who has indignation every day (Psalm 7, 11)."

"... the LORD sits enthroned for ever,
he has established his throne for judgment;
and he judges the world with righteousness,
he judges the peoples with equity (Psalms 9, 7,8)."

Again, the Hebrew perception of judgment as something good for the one being judged, as something longed for and sought after, comes out in Psalm 26. The Psalmist prays,

> "Judge me, O LORD, for I have walked in mine integrity, I have trusted also in the LORD; therefore I shall not slide.
> (Psalm 26, 1 KJV)."

In a modern translation, the connection is again made between judgment and vindication for the oppressed one:

> "Vindicate me, O LORD, for I have walked in my integrity, and I have trusted in the LORD without wavering
> (Psalm 26, 1 NRSV)."

> "Against you, you alone, have I sinned,
> and done what is evil in your sight,
> so that you are justified in your sentence
> and blameless when you pass judgment (Psalm 51, 4 NRSV)."

> " '... surely there is a God who judges on earth (Psalm 58, 11b).' "

> "God has taken his place in the divine council;
> in the midst of the gods he holds judgment ... (Psalm 82, 1)."

> "... it is God who executes judgment,
> putting down one and lifting up another (Psalm 75, 7)."

> "From the heavens you uttered judgment; the earth feared and was still when God rose up to establish judgment, to save all the oppressed of the earth (Psalm 76, 8-9 NRSV)."

> "Righteousness and justice are the foundation of your throne; steadfast love and faithfulness go before you (Psalm 89, 14 NRSV)

> "Rise up, O judge of the earth;
> render to the proud their deserts (Psalm 94, 2)!"

> "Say among the nations, The LORD reigns!
> Yea, the world is established, it

shall never be moved;
he will judge the peoples with
   equity."
Let the heavens be glad, and let
   earth rejoice;
let the sea roar, and all that fills it;
let the field exult, and everything
   in it!

Then shall all the trees of the wood
   sing for joy
before the LORD, for he comes,
   for he comes to judge the earth.
He will judge the world with
   righteousness,
and the peoples with his truth (Psalm 96, 10-13)."

"The LORD reigns; let the earth
   rejoice;
let the many coastlands be glad!
Clouds and thick darkness are
   round about him;
righteousness and justice are the
   foundation of his throne (Psalm 97, 1-2)."

"Mighty king, lover of justice,
   you have established equity;
you have executed justice
   and righteousness in Jacob (Psalm 99, 4 NRSV)."

"The LORD works vindication
   and justice for all who are
      oppressed (Psalm 103, 6 NRSV)."

"How long must your servant
      endure?
When will you judge those who
      persecute me (Psalm 119, 84 NRSV)?"

"The LORD is just in all his ways,
   and kind in all his doings (Psalm 145, 17)."

"He shall judge between the nations,
   and shall decide for many
      peoples;

and they shall beat their swords into
    plowshares,
and their spears into pruning
    hooks (Isaiah 2, 4)."

"... the LORD of hosts is exalted in
    justice,
and the Holy God shows
    himself holy in righteousness (Isaiah 5, 16)."

"In the path of your judgments,
O LORD, we wait for you;
your name and your renown
are the soul's desire (Isaiah 26, 8 NRSV)."

"Therefore the LORD waits to be
    gracious to you;
therefore he exalts himself to show
    mercy to you.
For the LORD is a God of justice;
    blessed are all those who wait for
        him (Isaiah 30, 18)."

"For the LORD is our judge, the LORD
    is our ruler,
the LORD is our king; he will save
    us (Isaiah 33, 22)."

"But you, O LORD of hosts, who
    judge righteously;
who try the heart and the mind,
let me see your retribution upon
    them,
for to you I have committed my
    cause (Jeremiah 11, 20 NRSV)."

" 'Therefore I will judge you, O house of Israel, every one according to his ways, says the LORD God (Ezekiel 18, 30a).' "

"... my judgment goes forth like the light (Hosea 6, 4c)."

" 'Let the nations bestir themselves... for ... I will sit to judge all the nations ... (Joel 3, 12).' "

"Then Jesus told them a parable about their need to pray always and not to lose heart. He said, 'In a certain city there was a judge who neither feared God nor had respect for people. In that city there was a widow who kept coming to him and saying, 'Grant me justice against my opponent.' For a while he refused; but later he said to himself, 'Though I have no fear if God and no respect for anyone, yet because this widow keeps bothering me, I will grant her justice, so that she may not wear me out by continually coming.' And the Lord said, 'Listen to what the unjust judge says. And will not God grant justice to his chosen ones who cry out to him day and night? Will he delay long in helping them? I tell you, he will quickly grant justice to them. And yet, when the Son of Man comes, will he find faith on the earth (Luke 18, 1-8 NRSV)?"

Jesus said, " 'I can do nothing on my own authority; as I hear, I judge; and my judgment is just, because I seek not my own will but the will of him who sent me (John 5, 30).' "

" 'The Father judges no one, but has given all judgment to the Son, that all may honor the Son, even as they honor the Father. For as the Father has life in himself, so he has granted the Son also to have life in himself, and has given him authority to execute judgment, because he is the Son of man (John 5, 22,23a,26-27).' "

Jesus said, "I do not judge anyone who hears my words and does not keep them, for I came not to judge the world, but to save the world. The one who rejects me and does not receive my word has a judge; on the last day the word that I have spoken will serve as judge, for I have not spoken on my own, but the Father who sent me has himself given me a commandment about what to say and what to speak. And I know that his commandment is eternal life. What I speak, therefore, I speak just as the Father has told me (John 12, 47-50 NRSV)."

" '... I will judge the nation which they serve,' said God ... (Acts 7, 7a)." This is reference to the time when the Israelites were in bondage to the Egyptians.

Jesus is "... the one ordained by God to judge the living and the dead ((Acts 10, 42b)."

"While God has overlooked the times of human ignorance, now he commands all people everywhere to repent, because he has fixed a day on which he will have the world judged in righteousness by a man whom he has appointed, and of this he has given assurance to all by raising him from the dead (Acts 17, 30-31 NRSV)."

"Therefore you have no excuse, whoever you are, when you judge others; for in passing judgment on another, you condemn yourself, because you, the judge, are doing the very same things. You say, 'We know that God's judgment on those who do such things is in accordance with truth.' Do you imagine, whoever you are, that when you judge those who do such things and yet do them yourself, you will escape the judgment of God? Or do you despise the riches of his kindness and forbearance and patience? Do you not realize that God's kindness is meant to lead you to repentance (Romans 2, 1-4 NRSV)?"

"All who have sinned without the law will also perish without the law, and all who have sinned under the law will be judged by the law (Romans 2, 12)."

"… God, through Jesus Christ, will judge the secret thoughts of all (Romans 2, 16b NRSV)."

"O the depth of the riches and wisdom and knowledge of God! How unsearchable are his judgments and how inscrutable his ways (Romans 11, 33)!"

"Why do you pass judgment on your brother or sister? Or you, why do you despise your brother of sister? For we will all stand before the judgment seat of God. For it is written, 'As I live ,says the Lord, every knee shall bow to me, and every tongue shall give praise to God.' So then each of us will be accountable to God (Romans 14, 10-12 NRSV)."

St. Paul says, "I do not even judge myself. I am not aware of anything against myself, but I am not thereby acquitted. It is the Lord who judges me. Therefore do not pronounce judgment before the time, before the Lord comes, who will bring to light the things now hidden in darkness and will disclose the purposes of the heart
(1 Corinthians 4, 3b-5a)."

The verb here is "anakrino," which has to do with investigating, interrogating, discerning, etc. Paul is saying that he is leaving all those activities to God.

"For what have I to do with judging outsiders? Is it not those inside the church whom you are to judge? God judges those outside. Drive out the wicked person from among you (1 Corinthians 5, 12-13)."

In this reference, the verb for "judging" is "krino" and is a judicial determination which may involve avenging, condemning, and imposing penalties.

"When any of you has a grievance against another, do you dare to take it to court before the unrighteous, instead of taking it before the saints? Do you not know that the saints will judge the world? And if the world is to be judged by you, are you incompetent to try trivial cases? Do you not know that we are to judge angels – to say nothing of ordinary matters? If you have ordinary cases, then, do you appoint as judges those who have no standing in the church? I say this to your shame. Can it be that there is no one among you wise enough to decide between one believer and another, but a believer goes to court against a believer – and before unbelievers at that (1 Corinthians 6, 1-7 NRSV)."

"For I received from the Lord what I also handed on to you, that the Lord Jesus on the night when he was betrayed took a loaf of bread, and when he had given thanks, he broke it and said, 'This is my body that is for you. Do this in remembrance of me.' In the same way he took the cup also, after supper, saying, 'This cup is the new covenant in my blood. Do this, as often as you drink it, in remembrance of me. For as often as you eat this bread and drink the cup, you proclaim the Lord's death until he comes. Whoever, therefore, eats the bread or drinks the cup of the Lord in an unworthy manner will be answerable for the body and blood of the Lord. Examine yourselves, and only then eat of the bread and drink of the cup. For all who eat and drink without discerning the body, eat and drink judgment against themselves. For this reason many of you are weak and ill, and some have died. But if we judged ourselves, we would not be judged. But when we are judged by the Lord, we are disciplined so that we may not be condemned along with the world
(1 Corinthians 11, 23-32 NRSV)."

In the previous context of 1 Corinthians 4, Paul is saying that he does not even judge himself; he leaves that up to God. In this context of the Lord's Supper, however, Paul stresses the need of self-examination.

"In the presence of God and of Christ Jesus, who is to judge the living and the dead, and in view of his appearing and his kingdom, I solemnly urge you: proclaim the message; be persistent whether the time is favorable or unfavorable; convince, rebuke, and encourage, with the utmost patience in teaching (2 Timothy 4, 1-2 NRSV)."

Paul, in the passage above, after delivering his charge to Timothy, turns to the subject of his own approaching death. "For I am already on the point of being sacrificed; the time of my departure has come. I have fought the good fight, I have finished the race, I have kept the faith. Henceforth there is laid up for me the crown of righteousness, which the Lord, the righteous judge, will award to me on that Day, and not only to me but also to all who have loved his appearing (2 Timothy 4, 6-8)."

"And just as it is appointed for mortals to die once, and after that, the judgment, so Christ, having been offered once to bear the sins of many, will appear a second time, not to deal with sin, but to save those who are eagerly waiting for him (Hebrews 9, 27-28 NRSV)."

In reading the Letter to the Hebrews, it is helpful to recall the connotations associated with the verb "judge." For us, there are perhaps fearful associations with the word.

However, the ancient Hebrew people longed for God's judgment. This was because they associated God's judgment with God's justice. If they had been mistreated, not to worry. GOD would intervene and "judge" on their behalf. We see this in Psalm 7, 8. David prays, "judge me, O LORD, according to my righteousness and according to the integrity that is in me."

The verb "judge" carries with it the sense of "vindicate."

"For we know the one who said, 'Vengeance is mine, I will repay.' And again, 'The LORD will judge his people
(Hebrews 10, 30 NRSV).' "

"... a judge who is God of all (Hebrews 12, 23b)."

"Let marriage be held in honor by all, and let the marriage bed be kept undefiled; for God will judge fornicators and adulterers.
(Hebrews 13, 4 NRSV)."

"So speak and so act as those who are to be judged under the law of liberty. For judgement is without mercy to one who has shown no mercy; yet mercy triumphs over judgment (James 2, 12-13)."

"Do not speak evil against one another, brothers and sisters. Whoever speaks evil against another or judges another, speaks evil against the law and judges the law; but if you judge the law, you are not a doer of the law but a judge. There is one lawgiver and judge who is able to save and to destroy. So who, then, are you to judge your neighbor (James 4, 11-12 NRSV)?"

"If you invoke as Father the one who judges all people impartially

according to their deeds, live in reverent fear during the time of your exile (1 Peter 1, 17 NRSV)."

Jesus is our example. "For to this you have been called, because Christ also suffered for you, leaving you an example, that you should follow in his steps. He committed no sin; no guile was found on his lips. When he was reviled, he did not revile in return; when he suffered, he did not threaten; but he trusted to him who judges justly (1 Peter 2, 21-23)."

"For if God did not spare the angels when they sinned, but cast them into hell and committed them to pits of nether gloom to be kept until the judgment; if he did not spare the ancient world, but preserved Noah, a herald of righteousness, with seven other persons, when he brought a flood upon the world of the ungodly; if by turning the cities of Sodom and Gomorrah to ashes he condemned them to extinction and made them an example to those who were ungodly; and if he rescued righteous Lot, greatly distressed by the licentiousness of the wicked (for by what that righteous man saw and heard as he lived among them, he was vexed in his righteous soul day after day with their lawless deeds), then the Lord knows how to rescue the godly from trial, and to keep the unrighteous under punishment until the day of judgment, and especially those who indulge in the lust of defiling passion and despise authority (2 Peter 2, 4-9)."

"First of all you must understand this, that in the last days scoffers will come, scoffing and indulging their own lusts and saying, 'Where is the promise of his coming? For ever since our ancestors died, all things continue as they were from the beginning of creation!' They deliberately ignore this fact, that by the word of God heavens existed long ago and an earth was formed out of water, through which the world of that time was deluged with water and perished. But by the same word the present heavens and earth have been reserved for fire, being kept until the day of judgment and destruction of the godless (2 Peter 3, 3-7 NRSV)."

The First Letter of John assures us that forgiveness is available. It is available, but it is not automatic. "If we say we have no sin, we deceive ourselves and the truth is not in us. If we confess our sins, he is faithful and just, and will forgive our sins and cleanse us from all unrighteousness (1 John 1, 8-9)."

"God abides in those who confess that Jesus is the Son of God, and they abide in God. So we have known and believe the love that God has for us. God is love, and those who abide in love abide in God, and God abides in them. Love has been perfected among us in this: that we may have boldness on the day of judgment, because as he is, so are we in the world (1 John 4, 15-17 NRSV)."

"Now I desire to remind you, though you are fully informed, that the LORD, who once for all saved a people out of the land of Egypt, afterwards destroyed those who did not believe. And the angels who did not keep their own position, but left their proper dwelling, he has kept in eternal chains in deepest darkness for the judgment of the great Day. Likewise Sodom and Gomorrah and the surrounding cities, which, in the same manner as they, in sexual immorality and pursued unnatural lust, serve as an example by undergoing a punishment of eternal fire (Jude 5-7 NRSV)."

"... Enoch in the seventh generation from Adam, prophesied, saying, 'See, the LORD is coming with ten thousands of his holy ones, to execute judgment on all, and to convict everyone of all the deeds of ungodliness that they have committed in such an ungodly way, and of all the harsh things that ungodly sinners have spoken against him (Jude 14, 15 NRSV)."

We turn now to a scene in heaven. The martyrs are crying out to God. "... 'Sovereign Lord, holy and true, how long will it be before you judge and avenge our blood on the inhabitants of the earth?' They were each given a white robe and told to rest a little longer, until the number would be complete both of their fellow servants and of their brothers and sisters who were soon to be killed as they themselves had been killed (Revelation 6, 9-11 NRSV)."

John, the writer of the Revelation, describes another scene in heaven, "And they sing the song of Moses, the servant of God, and the song of the Lamb, saying,

> 'Great and wonderful are thy deeds,
> O Lord God the Almighty!
> Just and true are thy ways,
> O King of the ages!
> Why shall not fear and glorify thy
>   name, O Lord?
> For thou alone art holy.
> All nations shall come and worship
>   thee,
> for thy judgments have been
>   revealed (Revelation 15, 3-4).' "

John continues with another scene in heaven,

> "Then I saw heaven opened, and behold, a white horse!
>   He who sat upon it is called Faithful and True,
>   and in righteousness he judges ... (Revelation 19, 11)."

Over and over it is emphasized that God's judgements are perfectly "fair," perfectly just. According to John,

"After this I heard what seemed to be the loud voice of a great multitude in heaven saying, 'Hallelujah! Salvation and glory and power to our God, for his judgments are true and just; he has judged the great whore who corrupted the earth with her fornication, and he has avenged on her the blood of his servants.' Once more they said, 'Hallelujah! The smoke goes up from her forever and ever.' And the twenty-four elders and the four living creatures fell down and worshiped God who is seated on the throne, saying, "Amen. Hallelujah (Revelation 19, 1-4 NRSV)!' "

KING

The ancient people of Israel were becoming jealous because the other nations had kings and they did not. God was their King, but they weren't satisfied; they wanted to be like the other nations and have a human, visible monarch.

Samuel, quiet and retiring, as far as prophets go, grew old and appointed his sons to rule as judges over Israel. Since his sons turned out to be corrupt, the elders of the people came to Samuel and protested,

"Behold, you are old and your sons do not walk in your ways; now appoint for us a king to govern us like all the nations. But the thing displeased Samuel when they said, 'Give us a king to govern us.' And Samuel prayed to the LORD. And the LORD said to Samuel, 'Hearken to the voice of the people in all that they say to you; for they have not rejected you, but they have rejected me from being king over them (1 Samuel 8, 4-7)."

The Lord told Samuel to warn the people of some of the implications restricting personal freedom which would occur if they were to have a human king. The people paid no attention to Samuel and still insisted. The Lord chose Saul, from the tribe of Benjamin, as king, and Samuel duly anointed him with oil.

Samuel recounted to the people how God had delivered them out the hands of the Egyptians and continued to act on behalf of his people. As Samuel said, "The LORD was your king." (1 Samuel 12, 12b) Although it was not in the best interest of the people to have a king, God decided to let them have their way. Even so, Samuel told them, "If both you and the king who reigns over you will follow the LORD your God, it will be well, but if you will not hearken to the voice of the LORD, but rebel against the commandments of the LORD, then the hand of the LORD will be against you and your king." (1 Samuel 12, 14b-15) Samuel reassures the people that, in spite of their choice, he will still be concerned for them and will pray for them. The books of Kings and Chronicles tell us what is was like for Israel to have kings. Some sincerely followed the Lord and others did not.

King David eloquently acknowledges the Lord's sovereignty in many psalms.

> "Let the heavens be glad,
>   and let the earth rejoice,
>   and let them say among the nations,
> 'The LORD reigns (1 Chronicles 16, 31)!' "

> "Hearken to the sound of my cry,
>   my King and my God,
>   for to thee do I pray (Psalm 5, 2)."

> "Lift up your heads, O gates!
>   and be lifted up, O ancient doors!
>   that the King of glory may come in.
>   Who is this King of glory?
>   The LORD, strong and mighty,
>   The LORD, mighty in battle!
>   Who is this King of glory?
>   The LORD of hosts,
>   He is the King of glory (Psalm 24, 7,8,10)."

> "The LORD sits enthroned over the flood;
>   The LORD sits enthoned as king for ever (Psalm 29, 10)."

Over and over throughout the Psalter, the Lord God is acknowledged and praised as King.

In the calling of the prophet Isaiah, the Lord is revealed as King.

> "In the year that King Uzziah died I saw the LORD
>   sitting upon a throne, high and lifted up; and his train
>   filled the temple. Above him stood the seraphim; each had six
>   wings: with two he covered his face, with two he covered his
>   feet, and with two he flew. And one called to another and
>   said,
>   'Holy, holy, holy is the LORD of hosts;
>   the whole earth is full of his glory.'
>
>   And the foundations of the thresholds shook at the voice
>   of him who called, and the house was filled with smoke. And I
>   said, 'Woe is me! For I am lost; for I am a man of unclean
>   lips, and I dwell in the midst of a people of unclean lips;

for my eyes have seen the King, the LORD of hosts!"

Then flew one of the seraphim to me, having in his hand
a burning coal which he had taken with tongs from the altar.
And he touched my mouth, and said, 'Behold, this has touched
your lips; your guilt is taken away and your sin forgiven.'
and I heard the voice of the LORD saying, 'Whom shall I send
and who will go for us? And I said, 'Here am I! Send me
(Isaiah 6, 1-8).' "

"Your eyes will see the king in his beauty;
they will behold a land that stretches afar.
Look upon Zion, the city of our appointed feasts!
Your eyes will see Jerusalem,
a quiet habitation, an immovable tent.
whose stakes will never be plucked up,
nor will any of its cords be broken.
But there the LORD in majesty will be there for us
a place of broad rivers and streams,
where no galley with oars can go,
nor stately ship can pass.
For the LORD is our judge, the LORD is our ruler,
the LORD is our king;
he will save us (Isaiah 33, 17, 20-22)."
"I am the LORD, your Holy One,
the Creator of Israel, your King (Isaiah 43, 15)."

There is great tenderness in this verse. The majestic God, the Mighty One, is called, not THE Holy One, but YOUR Holy One.

The tenderness of the lovers in the Song of Solomon ("My beloved is mine and I am his." (Song 2, 16) is seen here and in many other places in the Bible.

"There is none like thee, O LORD;
thou art great, and thy name is great in might.
Who would not fear thee, O King of the nations?
For this is thy due;
for among all the wise ones of the nations
and in all their kingdoms
there is none like thee (Jeremiah 10, 6-7)."

"... the LORD is the true God;
He is the living God and the everlasting King (Jeremiah 10, 10)."

King Nebuchadnezzar (he was the one who threw Shadrach,

Meschach, and Abednego in the fiery furnace) had been warned of a coming chastisement unless he acknowledged the sovereignty of God. After seven years of great affliction he said,

> "Now I, Nebuchadnezzar, praise and extol and honor the King of heaven; for all his works are just; and those who walk in pride he is able to abase (Daniel 4, 37)."

> "Rejoice greatly, O daughter Zion! Shout aloud, O daughter Jerusalem! Lo, your king comes to you; triumphant and victorious is he, humble and riding on a donkey, on a colt, the foal of a donkey (Zechariah 9, 9 NRSV)."

In the Gospels (John 12, 14-15 and Matthew 21, 5), this passage from Zechariah was quoted shortly before Jesus entered Jerusalem prior to his crucifixion.

The prophecy above refers to the first coming of Christ, as the gentle, humble One.

Zechariah also prophesied of Christ's return as triumphant, reigning King:

> "And the LORD will become King over all the earth;
> on that day the LORD will be one and his name one.
> Then every one that survives of all the nations that
> have come against Jerusalem shall go up year after year
> to worship the King, the LORD of hosts,
> and to keep the feast of booths (Zechariah 14, 9, 16)."

Turning now to the New Testament, we see Jesus, very early, acknowledged as King. The jealous despot, King Herod, pretended interest in the newborn infant. "Now when Jesus was born in Bethlehem of Judea in the days of Herod the king, behold wise men from the East came to Jerusalem, saying, 'Where is he who has been born king of the Jews? For we have seen his star in the East, and have come to worship him.' When Herod the king heard this, he was troubled, and all Jerusalem with him; and assembling all the chief priests and scribes of the people, he inquired of them where the Christ was to be born. They told him, 'In Bethlehem of Judea; for so it is written by the prophet:

> 'And you, O Bethlehem, in the land of Judah,
> are by no means least among the rulers of Judah,
> for from you shall come a ruler
> who will govern my people
> Israel (Matthew 2, 1-6).'"

Herod, of course, sent the wise men on to Bethlehem and instructed them to notify him when they had found Jesus. The wise men were warned in a dream not to do so. In retaliation, the enraged Herod ordered the murder of all the little boys two years old and under who lived in or near Bethlehem. The slaughter of these innocents had been foretold by the prophet Jeremiah:

> " 'Thus says the LORD:
> 'A voice is heard in Ramah,
> lamentation and bitter weeping.
> Rachel is weeping for her children;
> she refuses to be comforted
> for her children,
> because they are not (Jeremiah 31, 15).' "

Matthew portrays Jesus, not only as the gentle king riding a humble donkey into Jerusalem, but also as the triumphant king who will judge the nations:

> "When the Son of man comes in his glory, and all the angels with him, then he will sit on his glorious throne. Before him will be gathered all the nations, and he will separate them one from another as a shepherd separates the sheep from the goats, and he will place the sheep at his right hand, but the goats at the left. Then the King will say to those at his right hand, 'Come, O blessed of my Father, inherit the kingdom prepared for you from the foundation of the world; for
>
> I was hungry and you gave me food,
> I was thirsty and you gave me drink,
> I was a stranger and you welcomed me,
> I was naked and you clothed me,
> I was sick and you visited me,
> I was in prison and you came to me.'

Then the righteous will answer him,

> 'Lord, when did we see thee hungry and feed thee,
> or thirsty and give thee drink?
> And when did we see thee a stranger and welcome thee,
> or naked and clothe thee?
> And when did we see thee sick
> or in prison and visit thee?'

And the King will answer them,

'Truly, I say to you, as you did it to one of the least of these my brethren, you did it to me (Matthew 25, 31-40).' "

In all four Gospels, in his interrogation before Pilate, Jesus is asked the question, "Are you the King of the Jews?" (Matthew 27, 11, Mark 15, 2, Luke 23, 3, John 19, 33) In Matthew, Mark, and Luke, the synoptic gospels, Jesus answers, "You have said so." In the Fourth Gospel, he answers,

" 'Do you say this of your own accord, or did others say it to you about me? Pilate answered, 'Am I a Jew? Your own nation and the chief priests have handed you over to me; what have you done? Jesus answered, 'My kingship is not of this world; if my kingship were of this world, my servants would fight ... 'Pilate said to him, 'So you are a king?' Jesus answered, 'You say that I am a king. For this I was born, and for this I have come into the world, to bear witness to the truth. Every one who is of the truth hears my voice (John 18, 34-37).' "

"Then the soldiers of the government took Jesus into the praetorium, and they gathered the whole battalion before him. And they stripped him and put a scarlet robe upon him, and plaiting a crown of thorns they put it on his head, and put a reed in his right hand. And kneeling before him, they mocked him, saying, 'Hail, King of the Jews!' And they spat upon him, and took the reed and struck him on the head. And when they had mocked him, they stripped him of the robe, and put his own clothes upon him, and led him away to crucify him
(Matthew 27, 27-31)."

Any suffering or injustice we may be called upon to endure cannot be compared to that of Our Lord and Savior being mocked by those He loved and came to save.

The mocking continued after He was crucified. "And over his head they put the charge against him, which read, 'This is Jesus the King of the Jews. 'Then two robbers who were crucified with him, one on the right and one on the left. And those who passed by derided him, wagging their heads and saying, 'You who would destroy the temple and build it in three days, save yourself! If you are the Son of God, come down from the cross.' So also the chief priests, with the scribes and elders, mocked him, saying, 'He saved others; he cannot save himself. He is the King of Israel; let him come down now from the cross, and we will believe in him. He trusts in God; let God deliver him now, if he desires him; for he said, 'I am the Son of God.' " And the robbers who were crucified with him also reviled him in the same way (Matthew 27, 37-44)."

Jesus was by no means powerless, but He chose to limit His sovereignty in order to accomplish His great work of redemption for us. Earlier he had said, "Do you think I cannot appeal to my Father, and he will at once send me more than twelve legions of angels? But how then should the scriptures be fulfilled, that it must be so (Matthew 26, 53-54)."

Do you know how many angels that would be? Seventy-two thousand! The actual number is not as important as is the underlying truth that, again, it was of His own free will that Our Lord died on our behalf.

It seemed that the powers of darkness had the last word. Not so!

God "raised him from the dead and made him sit at his right hand in the heavenly places, far above all rule and authority and power and dominion, and above every name that is named, not only in this age but also in that which is to come; and he has put all things under his feet and has made him the head over all things for the church, which is his body, the fullness of him who fills all in all (Ephesians 1, 20-23)."

Jesus, who will return as our glorious King, first humbled himself. "Let this mind be in you that was in Christ Jesus, who, though he was in the form of God, did not regard equality with God as something to be exploited, but emptied himself, taking the form of a slave, being born in human likeness, And being found in human form, he humbled and became obedient to the point of death – even death on a cross. Therefore God also highly exalted him and gave him the name that is above every name, so that at the name of Jesus every knee should bend, in heaven and on earth, and every tongue confess that Jesus Christ is Lord, to the glory of God the Father (Philippians 2, 3-11 NRSV).

In the first letter to Timothy, St. Paul refers to Jesus as "the King eternal, immortal, invisible, the only God" (1 Timothy 1, 17) and "the blessed and only Sovereign, the King of kings and Lord of lords, who alone has immortality and dwells in unapproachable light …
(1 Timothy 6, 15-16)."

Over and over in the book of the Revelation, Jesus is acknowledged as King. "And they sang the song of Moses, the servant of God, and the song of the Lamb, saying,

> 'Great and wonderful are thy deeds,
> O Lord God the Almighty!
> Just and true are thy ways,
> O King of the ages!
> Who shall not fear and glorify thy

name, O Lord?
For thou alone art holy.
All nations shall come and worship
  thee,
for thy judgments have been
  revealed (Revelation 14, 3-4).' "

"... they will make war on the Lamb, and the Lamb will conquer them, for he is Lord of lords and King of kings, and those with him are called and chosen and faithful."
(Revelation 17, 14)

LAMB

The Lamb of God (Agnus Dei) is one of my own most beloved images of Our Lord. From the very first book of the Bible, Genesis, the lamb has been the symbol of sacrificial love. Our home is full of lambs! There is a stained glass Lamb of God, paintings of shepherdesses and lambs, lamb cards, stuffed wooly lambs, etc. And then there is Gianna!

Do you remember the story of God's testing of Abraham? God wanted to find out if Abraham would obey Him at all costs, so He told Abraham to sacrifice his only son, Isaac. How could God ask this, since all future promises seemed to hinge on Isaac? God had previously said to Abraham, "Sarah your wife shall bear you a son, and you shall call his name Isaac. I will establish my covenant with him as an everlasting covenant for his descendants after him." (Genesis 17, 19). In due time Isaac was born. How in the world could God ask this? With a heavy heart, Abraham set out with Isaac, the wood, and the fire. Isaac must have wondered what was going on! He asked, "Behold the fire and the wood; but where is the lamb for a burnt offering?" (Genesis 22, 7) Remember, Abraham still had no idea of what was going to happen. He was determined to obey God at all costs. He answered his son, "God will provide himself the lamb for a burnt offering, my son." (Genesis 22, 8) And you know the rest of the story. Abraham bound Isaac, laid him on the altar, and was about to kill him, when the angel of the Lord intervened and said, "Do not lay your hand on the lad or do anything to him; for now I know that you fear God, seeing you have not withheld your son, your only son, from me." (Genesis 22, 12) Abraham then saw a ram caught in a thicket to be the burnt offering. People in that day were big into naming places, so Abraham named that memorable place, "The LORD will provide." Not only did the Lord provide the offering, but it was the Lord Himself who intervened.

The next mention of a sacrificial lamb was at the time of the first Passover. God was gearing up to deliver his chosen people in a big way! The Egyptians had tyrannized over them long enough. After a few plagues, their ruler, the Pharoah, still refused to release the Israelites. So God said to Moses, "Yet one plague more I will bring upon Pharoah and upon Egypt; afterwards he will let you go ... (Exodus 11, 1)."

Small wonder. This time, at midnight, all the first-born in the land of Egypt would die. God gave precise instructions to Moses and Aaron.

The Lord said, "Tell the whole congregation of Israel that on the tenth of this month they are to take a lamb for each family, a lamb for each household. If a household is too small for a whole lamb, it shall join its closest neighbor in obtaining one; the lamb shall be divided in proportion to the number of people who eat it. Your lamb shall be without blemish, a year-old male; you may take it from the sheep or from the goats. You shall keep it until the fourteenth day of this month; then the whole assembled congregation of Israel shall slaughter it at twilight. They shall take some of the blood and put it on the two doorposts and the lintel of the houses in which they eat it. They shall eat the lamb that same night; they shall eat it roasted over the fire with unleavened bread and bitter herbs. This is how you shall eat it; your loins girded, your sandals on your feet, and your staff in your hand; and you shall eat it hurriedly. It is the passover of the LORD. For I will pass through the land of Egypt that night, and I will strike down every firstborn in the land of Egypt, both human beings and animals; on all the gods of Egypt I will execute judgments: I am the LORD. The blood shall be a sign for you on the houses where you live: when I see the blood, I will pass over you, and no plague shall destroy you when I strike the land of Egypt (Exodus 12, 3-8. 11-13 NRSV)."

Lambs were, of course, significant in the ordination of priests. After the seven day ordination ceremony of Aaron and his sons, also priests, the Lord, on the eighth day, gave instructions regarding sacrifices.

The whole idea behind the sacrifice of lambs and other animals was to show that the innocent suffer and die for the guilty. The book of Leviticus elaborates on this in the descriptions of sin offerings, burnt offerings, and peace offerings.

Jesus was the Lamb of God. His was the ultimate sacrifice. God became a human being and offered himself -- his very life -- to take away our sins. There were hints of this in the book of Isaiah.

"He was despised and rejected by others; a man of suffering and acquainted with infirmity; as one from whom others hide their faces he was despised, and we held him of no account. Surely he has borne our infirmities and carried our diseases; yet we accounted him stricken, struck down by God and afflicted. But he was wounded for our transgressions, crushed for our iniquities; upon him was the punishment that made us whole, and by his bruises we are healed. All we like sheep have gone astray; we have all turned to our own way, and the LORD has laid on him the iniquity of us all. He was oppressed, and he was afflicted, yet he did not open his mouth; like a lamb that is led to the slaughter, and like a sheep that before its shearers is silent, so he did not open his mouth (Isaiah 53, 3-7 NRSV)."

John the Baptist, who has been called the last of the Old Testament prophets, was keenly cognizant of his own role -- that of preparing the way of the Lord Jesus. One day he saw Jesus walking towards him and said,

"Behold the Lamb of God, who takes away the sins of the world (John 1, 29)!"

The First Letter of Peter was written to encourage the suffering Christians of Asia Minor:

"Therefore prepare your minds for action; discipline yourselves; set all your hope on the grace that Jesus Christ will bring you when he is revealed. Like obedient children, do not be conformed to the desires that you formerly had in ignorance. Instead, as he who called you is holy, be holy yourselves in all your conduct; for it is written, 'You shall be holy, for I am holy.' If you invoke as Father the one who judges all people impartially according to their deeds, live in reverent fear during the time of your exile. You know that you were ransomed from the futile ways inherited from your ancestors, not with perishable things like silver of gold, but with the precious blood of Christ, like that of a lamb without defect or blemish. He was destined before the foundation of the world, but was revealed at the end of the ages for your sake. Through him you have come to trust in God, who raised him from the dead and gave him glory, so that your faith and hope are set on God
(1 Peter 1, 13-21 NRSV)."

It is in the Book of the Revelation of St. John that we find the most references to Jesus as the Lamb of God. This is no longer Jesus as the suffering and slain Lamb; this is Jesus the triumphant, risen Lamb. In the fifth chapter of the book, we are given a glimpse into heaven:

"... I saw a Lamb standing as though it had been slain .... The four living creatures and the twenty-four elders fell down before the Lamb, each holding a harp, and with golden bowls full of incense, which are the prayers of the saints; and they sang a new song, saying,

> 'Worthy art thou to take the scroll
> and to open its seals,
> for thou wast slain and by thy blood
> didst ransom for God
> from every tribe and tongue and
> people and nation,
> and hast made them a kingdom and
> priests to our God,
> and they shall reign on earth.'

Then I looked, and I heard around the throne and the living creatures and the elders the voices of many angels, numbering myriads of myriads and thousands of thousands, saying with a loud voice,

> 'Worthy is the Lamb who was slain,
> to receive power and wealth
> and wisdom and might and
> honor and glory and blessing!'

And I heard every creature in heaven and on earth and under the earth and in the sea, and all therein, saying,

> 'To him who sits upon the throne and to the Lamb
> be blessing and honor and glory and might for
> ever and ever (Revelation 5, 6-13).' "

Christ the Lamb who suffers is also Christ the Lamb who conquers. In the very next chapter of the Revelation, there is the cry from the mighty of the earth who are experiencing judgment. They even cry out to the mountains,

> "Fall on us and hide us from the face of him who is seated
> on the throne, and from the wrath of the Lamb; for
> the great day of their wrath has come, and who can stand
> before it (Revelation 6, 16-17)?"

In an interlude passage, the people of God are promised protection from the judgment falling upon those who refuse to believe.

> "After this I looked, and there was a great multitude
> that no one could count, from every nation,
> from all tribes and peoples and languages,
> standing before the throne and
> before the Lamb,

robed in white, with palm branches in their hands.
They cried out in a loud voice, saying

'Salvation belongs to our God who is seated upon the throne,
and to the Lamb!'

And all the angels stood around the throne and around the elders and the four living creatures, and they fell on their faces before the throne and worshipped God, singing,

'Amen! Blessing and glory and wisdom and
thanksgiving and honor and power and might
be to our God for ever and ever! Amen.'

Then one of the elders addressed me (John) saying, 'Who are these, robed in white, and where have they come from?' I said to him, 'Sir, you are the one that knows.' And he said to me, 'These are they who have come out of the great ordeal; they have washed their robes and made them white in the blood of the Lamb. For this reason they are they before the throne of God, and worship him day and night within his temple; and the one who is seated on the throne will shelter them. They will hunger no more, and thirst no more; the sun will not strike them, nor any scorching heat; for the Lamb at the center of the throne will be their shepherd, and he will guide them to springs of the water of life, and God will wipe away every tear from their eyes
(Revelation 7, 9-17 NRSV).' "

The conflict between Christ and Satan is described by John.

"Then I heard a loud voice in heaven, proclaiming, 'Now have come the salvation and the power and the kingdom of our God and the authority of his Messiah, for the accuser of our comrades has been thrown down, who accuses them day and night before our God. But they have conquered him by the blood of the Lamb and by the word of their testimony, for they did not cling to life even in the face of death. Rejoice then, you heavens and those who dwell in them! But woe to the earth and the sea, for the devil has come down to you with great wrath, because he knows that his time is short (Revelation 12, 10-12 NRSV)!' "

Satan ("the beast") was then allowed a limited time to exercise power and even to wage war on the saints of God. "And all who dwell on earth will worship it ("the beast"), every one whose name is not written in the book of life of the Lamb that was slain (Revelation 13, 8)."

In another interlude vision, the Lamb appears on Mount Zion with the redeemed. Again, God's people are being reassured that they will be cared for by their shepherd who is the Lamb (Rev. 14, 1-13)."

The battle waxes again between Christ the Lamb and powers of evil. "And they will wage war on the Lamb, and the Lamb will conquer them, for he is Lord of lords and King of kings, and those with him are called and chosen and faithful (Revelation 17, 14)."

John describes the scene in heaven after the victory of the Lamb.

"Then I heard what seemed to be the voice of a great multitude, like the sound of many waters and like the sound of mighty thunder peals, crying out, 'Hallelujah! For the Lord our God the Almighty reigns. Let us rejoice and exult an give him the glory, for the marriage of the Lamb has come, and his bride has made herself ready; to her it has been granted to be clothed with fine linen, bright and pure' – for the fine linen is the righteous deeds of the saints. And the angel said to me, "Write this" Blessed are those who are invited to the marriage supper of the Lamb.' And he said to me, 'These are true words of God
(Revelation 9, 6-9 NRSV).' "

John is granted further visions of "the Bride, the wife of the Lamb," and the "holy city Jerusalem coming down out of heaven from God, having the glory of God its radiance...." (Rev. 21, 9-11) There was no temple in the heavenly city, "for its temple is the Lord God the Almighty and the Lamb. And the city has no need of sun or moon to shine upon it, for the glory of God is its light and its lamp is the Lamb. By its light shall the nations walk; and the kings of the earth shall bring their glory into it, and its gates shall never be shut by day -- and there shall be no night there; and they shall bring into it the glory and the honor of the nations. But nothing unclean shall enter it, nor any one who practices abominations or falsehood, but only those who are written in the Lamb's book of life (Revelation 21, 22-27)."

The final reference to the Lamb is in the following chapter, which continues the description of heaven.

"... the river of life, bright as crystal, flowing from the throne of God and of the Lamb, through the middle of the street of the city; also, on either side of the river, the tree of life with its twelve kinds of fruit, yielding its fruit each month; and the leaves of the tree were for the healing of the nations.

There shall be no more anything accursed, but the throne of God and of the Lamb shall be in it, and his servants shall worship him; they shall see his face, and his name shall be on their foreheads. And night shall be no more; they need no light or lamp or sun, for the Lord God will be their light, and they shall reign for ever and ever (Revelation 22, 1-5)."

LAWGIVER

"For the LORD is our judge,
 the LORD is our lawgiver,
 the LORD is our king;
 he will save us (Isaiah 33, 22 KJV)."

"There is one lawgiver and judge;
 he who is able to save and to destroy.
 But who are you that you judge your neighbor (James 4, 12)?"

LEADER

"God exalted him (Jesus) at his right hand as Leader and Savior, to give repentance to Israel and forgiveness of sins (Acts 5, 31)."

LIFE

Not only does God give us life, but, in actuality, He is our very life.

"Jesus said .... 'I am the way, the truth, and the life;
 no one comes to the Father, but by me (John 14, 6)."

Jesus gives eternal life, in the sense of a relationship that transcends death, right now while we're still on this earth. When Lazarus died, his sisters, Mary and Martha, both knew that if Jesus had been around, their brother would not have died. They were in for a surprise! Before he raised Lazarus from the dead, he said,

'I am the resurrection and the life,
 he who believes in me, though he die, yet shall he live, and
 whoever lives and believes in me shall never die
  (John 11, 25,26).' "

"Set your minds on things that are above, not on the things that are on earth. For you have died, and your life is hid with Christ in God. When Christ who is our life appears, then you also will appear with him in glory (Colossians 3, 4)."

LIGHT

"The LORD is my light and my salvation;
  whom shall I fear?
The LORD is the stronghold of my life;
  of whom shall I be afraid (Psalm 27, 1)?"

"For with thee is the fountain of life;
  and in thy light do we see light (Psalm 36, 9)."

"Blessed are the people who know the festal shout,
  who walk, O LORD, in the light of thy countenance,
  who exult in thy name all the day,
  and extol thy righteousness (Psalm 89, 15)."

"The sun shall no more be your light by day,
  nor for brightness shall the moon
  give light to you by night;
  but the LORD will be your everlasting light,
  and your God will be your glory.
  Your sun shall no more go down,
  nor your moon withdraw itself;
  for the LORD will be your everlasting light,
  and your days of mourning shall be ended (Isaiah 60, 19-20)."

"Rejoice not over me, O my enemy;
  when I fall, I shall rise;
  when I sit in darkness,
  the LORD will be a light for me (Micah 7, 8)."

Mary and Joseph took the infant Jesus to the Temple to be dedicated to the Lord. The aged Simeon held the Child in his arms and said,

"Lord, now lettest thou thy servant
  depart in peace,
  according to thy word;
  for mine eyes have seen thy
  salvation
  which thou hast prepared in the presence
  of all peoples,
  a light for revelation to the Gentiles,
  and for glory to thy people Israel (Luke 22-32)!"

The beautiful Prologue to the Gospel of Saint John describes the Incarnation of the Lord Jesus, describing him as the "true light."

"In the beginning was the Word, and the Word was with God and the Word was God. He was in the beginning with God; all things were made through him, and without him was not anything made that was made. In him was life, and the life was the light of men. The light shines in the darkness, and the darkness has not overcome it.

There was a man sent from God, whose name was John. He came for testimony, to bear witness to the light, that all might believe through him. He was not the light, but came to bear witness to the light.

The true light that enlightens every man was coming into the world. He was in the world, and the world was made through him, yet the world knew him not. He came to his own home, and his own people received him not. But to all who received him, who believed in his name, he gave power to become children of God; who were born, not of blood nor of the will of the flesh nor of the will of man but of God.

And the Word became flesh and dwelt among us, full of grace and truth; we have beheld his glory, glory as of the only Son from the Father. (John bore witness to him, and cried, 'This was he of whom I said, 'He who comes after me ranks before me, for he was before me.') And from his fulness have we all received grace upon grace. For the law was given through Moses; grace and truth came through Jesus Christ (John 1, 1-18a)."

Jesus said, "I am the light of the world. Whoever follows me will never walk in darkness but will have the light of light (John 8, 12 NRSV)."

"As long as I am in the world, I am the light of the world (John 9, 5)."

"I have come as light into the world, that whoever believes in me may not remain in darkness (John 12, 46)."

"This is the message we have heard ... and proclaim to you, that God is light and in him is no darkness at all. If we say we have fellowship with him while we walk in darkness, we lie and do not live according to the truth; but if we walk in the light, as he is in the light we have fellowship with one another, and the blood of Jesus his Son cleanses us from all sin. If we say we have no sin, we deceive ourselves, and the truth is not in us. If we confess our sins, he is faithful and just and will forgive our sins and cleanse us from all unrighteousness (1 John 1, 5-9)."

In his heavenly vision, the writer of the Book of the Revelation describes the new Jerusalem. "And I saw no temple in the city, for its temple is the Lord God Almighty and the Lamb. And the city has no need of sun or moon to shine upon it, for the glory of God is its light, and its lamp is the Lamb (Revelation 21, 22-23)."

For those in heaven, "night shall be no more, they need no light of lamp or sun, for the Lord God will be their light, and they shall reign for ever and ever (Revelation 22, 5)."

LION

The Lord is compared to a lion in the book of the prophet Hosea.

> "I am the LORD your God
> from the land of Egypt;
> you know no God but me,
> and besides me there is no savior.
> It was I who knew you in the wilderness,
> in the land of drought;
> but when they had fed to the full,
> they were filled up, and their heart
> was lifted up;
> therefore they forgot me.
> So I will be to them like a lion ... (Hosea 13, 4-7a)."

In the Book of the Revelation, Jesus is often referred to as the Lamb. He is also referred to as the Lion.

"... the Lion of the tribe of Judah, the Root of David,
has conquered ... (Revelation 5, 5)."

THE LIVING GOD

The verses referring to the "living" God are not so much for purposes of nomenclature as they are for stressing the present reality of God. This is not some "good person," or "teacher," or even "prophet." This is the eternal, living God.

Jesus asked his disciples to tell him who people thought he was. "And they said, 'Some say John the Baptist, others say Elijah, and others Jeremiah or one of the prophets.' He said to them, 'But who do you say that I am?' Simon Peter replied, 'ou are the Christ, the Son of the living God (Matthew 16, 14-16).'"

Jesus reminded his Jewish listeners, "Very truly, I tell you, whoever believes has eternal life. I am the bread of life. Your ancestors ate the manna in the wilderness, and they died. This is the bread that comes down from heaven, so that one may eat of it and not die. I am the living bread that came down from heaven. Whoever eats of this bread will live forever; and the bread that I will give for the life of the world is my flesh (John 6, 47-51 NRSV).' "

In the Roman colony of Lystra, the people wanted to fall down and worship Paul and Barnabas. The apostles were horrified and said, "Why are you doing this? We also are men, of like nature with you, and bring you good news, that you should turn from these vain things to a living God who made the heaven and the earth and the sea and all that is in them (Acts 14, 15)."

Paul refers to the Corinthian Christians as a living "letter" to be read by all. "You yourselves are our letter, written on our hearts, to be known and read by all; and you show that you are a letter of Christ, prepared by us, written not with ink but with the Spirit of the living God, not on tablets of stone but on tablets of human hearts
(2 Corinthian 3, 2-3 NRSV)."

Paul goes on to advise the Christians in Corinth about their relationship with the pagans around them. "What agreement has the temple of God with idols? For we are the temple of the living God; as God said, 'I will live in them and walk among them, and I will be their God, and they shall be my people. Therefore come out from them, and be separate from them, says the Lord, and touch nothing unclean; then I will welcome you, and I will be your father, and you shall be my sons and daughters, says the Lord Almighty (2 Corinthians 6, 16-18 NRSV).' "

Paul reminds the Thessalonians of their of their conversion to Christ. "For the people of those regions report about us what kind of welcome we had among you, and how you turned to God from idols, to serve a living and true God, and to wait for his Son from heaven, who he raised from the dead – Jesus, who rescues us from the wrath that is coming (1 Thessalonians 1, 9-10 NRSV)."

The Letter of St. Paul to Timothy defines and describes the Church. "... the household of God, which is the church of the living God, the pillar and bulwark of the truth (1 Timothy 3, 15)."

" For to this end we toil and struggle, because we have our hope set on the living God, who is the Savior of all people, especially of those who believe (1 Timothy 4, 10 NRSV)."

The writer to the Hebrews contrasts the worship of heaven with the worship of earth: "For if the sprinkling of defiled persons with the blood of goats and bulls and with the ashes of a heifer sanctifies for the purification of the flesh, how much more shall the blood of Christ, who through the eternal Spirit offered himself without blemish to God, purify your conscience from dead works to serve the living God (Hebrews 9, 13-14)."

The two covenants -- old and new -- are contrasted. Moses received the old covenant at Mount Sinai.

In contrast, "... you have come to Mount Zion and to the city of the living God, the heavenly Jerusalem, and to innumerable angels in festal God the judge of all, and to the spirits of the righteous made perfect, and to Jesus, the mediator of a new covenant ... (Hebrews 12, 22-24a NRSV)."

THE LORD

There are, of course, many, many references in the Scriptures which refer to "the Lord." Jehovah, meaning the self-existent One or the eternal One, is the Jewish "national" name for God.

"Adonai" was another name for "Lord" or "sovereign," sometimes used in the human sense ("My LORD Moses," Numbers 11, 28).

In the New Testament, we find the Greek word "kurios" being used for "Lord" or for one whose authority is supreme.

The name "Lord" is first used in Genesis 2, 4 in describing the work of the creation of the earth and the heavens. "Then the LORD God formed man of dust from the ground, and breathed into his nostrils the breath of life; and man became a living being (Genesis 2, 7)." The chapter continues to describe in detail the Lord God's work of creation.

There are "specialized" names, such as "Jehovah-jireh" or "The LORD will provide" or "The LORD will see it." This particular name is the one used in the account of the testing of Abraham. As Abraham was about to sacrifice Isaac, the angel of the Lord (believed by some to be the pre-incarnate Christ) called to him to stop. Abraham then saw the ram which God had provided for the sacrifice.

"So Abraham called the name of that place 'The LORD will provide,' as it is said to this day, 'On the mount of the LORD it shall be provided (Genesis 22, 14).'"

This aspect of the Lord's provision is reflected in the letter to the Philippians: "And my God will supply every need of yours according to his riches in glory in Christ Jesus (Philippians 4, 19)."

The name "the LORD" is first introduced in the book of Exodus. "And God said to Moses, 'I am the LORD. I appeared to Abraham, to Isaac, and to Jacob, as God Almighty, but by my name the LORD I did not make myself known to them (Exodus 6, 2,3).'"

Another of the "specialized" names is Jehovah-Raphah or "I am the LORD your healer." The Lord said to the people of Israel during their time in the wilderness, " 'If you will diligently hearken to the voice of the LORD your God, and do that which is right in his eyes, and give heed to his commandments and keep all his statutes, I will put none of the diseases upon you which I put upon the Egyptians; for I am the LORD your healer (Exodus 15, 26).'"

This word "raphah" which refers to healing is quite interesting. There is the sense of healing or mending by stitching. The Lord is patiently and lovingly stitching you back together and making you whole.

Another name is Jehovah-Nissi, "The LORD is my Banner." This refers to an altar Moses built in the desert after the people finally defeated the fierce Amalakites. The New Jerusalem translates this verse (Exodus 17, 15) as "Lay hold of Yahweh's banner!"

Jehovah-Shalom, "The LORD is Peace," is yet another of these names. This was also the name of an altar. After Gideon was given the power to drive out the Midianites, he built an altar and called it "The LORD is Peace." (Judges 6, 24)

The name, "The LORD is Peace" is fulfilled in the life and ministry of Jesus. After His resurrection, He said to His disciples, "Peace be with you. As the Father has sent me, even so I send you (John 20, 21)."

Not only does Jesus give us peace, He IS our peace: "For he is our peace ... (Ephesians 2, 14)."

Another name is "The LORD our Righteousness." (Jeremiah 23, 6) God "... is the source of your life in Christ Jesus, who became for us wisdom from God, and righteousness and sanctification and redemption, in order that, as it is written, 'Let the one who boasts, boast in the Lord (1 Corinthians 1, 30-31 NRSV).'"

There are many references to "The LORD of Hosts."

"O great and mighty God whose name is the LORD of hosts,
   great in counsel and
      mighty in deed … (Jeremiah 32, 18-19)."

"For lo, the one who forms the mountains, creates the wind, reveals his thoughts to mortals, makes the morning darkness, and treads on the heights of the earth – the LORD, the God of hosts, is his name (Amos 4, 13 NRSV)!"

He is the ultimate Lord, especially in the descriptions in the book of Revelation.

"… King of kings and Lord of lords (Revelation 19, 16)."

"One thing have I desired of the LORD, which I will require; even that I may dwell in the house of the LORD all the days of my life, to behold the fair beauty of the LORD, and to visit his temple (Psalm 27, 4, Coverdale Translation, the old Book of Common Prayer p. 372)

MAJESTY

"Long ago God spoke to our ancestors in many and various ways by the prophets, but in these last days he has spoken to us by a Son, whom he appointed heir of all things, through whom he also created the worlds. He is the reflection of God's glory and the exact imprint of God's very being, and he sustains all things by his powerful word. When he had made purification for sins, he sat down at the right hand of the Majesty on high (Hebrews 1, 1-3 NRSV)."

"For we did not follow cleverly devised myths when we made known to you the power and coming of our Lord Jesus Christ, but we were eyewitnesses of his majesty. For when he received honor and glory from God the Father and the voice was borne to him by the Majestic Glory,

   'This is my beloved Son, with whom I am well pleased,'
   we heard this voice borne from heaven, for we were with
   him on the holy mountain (2 Peter 1-16-18)."

MAKER

Elihu, the only one of Job's friends whom God does not rebuke, defends the ways of God.

" 'Bear with me a little, and I will show you,
for I have yet something to say on God's behalf.
I will fetch my knowledge from afar,
and ascribe righteousness to my Maker (Job 36, 2-3).' "

"O come, let us worship and bow down,
let us kneel before the LORD, our Maker!
For he is our God,
and we are the people of his pasture,
and the sheep of his hand (Psalm 95, 6-7)."

"Those who oppress the poor insult
    their Maker,
but those who are kind to the
    needy honor him (Proverbs 14, 31 NRSV)."

"Woe to you who strive with your Maker,
earthen vessels with the potter!
Does the clay say to the one who fashions it,
'What are you making'? or
'Your work has no handles'?
Woe to anyone who says to a father,
'What are you begetting?'
or to a woman,
With what are you in labor?'

Thus says the LORD,
the Holy One of Israel, and its
  Maker:
'Will you question me about my children,
  or command me concerning the work of my hands?
I made the earth,
  and created humankind upon it;
it was my hands that stretched out
  the heavens,
and I commanded all their host (Isaiah 45, 9-12 NRSV).' "

God is not only your Maker. God is also your "re-maker" who can re-make your life. "I, I am he who comforts you; why then are you afraid of a mere mortal who must die, a human being who fades like grass? You have forgotten the LORD, your Maker, who stretched out the heavens and laid the foundations of the earth (Isaiah 51, 12-13a NRSV)."

"... your Maker is your husband,
the LORD of hosts is his name;
and the Holy One of Israel is your

Redeemer,
the God of the whole earth he is called (Isaiah 54, 5)."

In the book of the Revelation, the Lord says,

"Behold, I make all things new (Revelation 21, 5a KJV)."

MASTER (Teacher)

"And a certain scribe came, and said unto him, Master, I will follow thee whithersoever thou goest. And Jesus saith unto him, The foxes have holes, and the birds of the air have nests; but the Son of man hath not where to lay his head (Matthew 8, 19-20 KJV)."

"A scribe then approached and said, 'Teacher, I will follow you wherever you go.' And Jesus said to him, Foxes have holes, and birds of the air have nests; but the Son of Man has nowhere to lay his head (Matthew 8, 19-20 NRSV)."

In this passage from Matthew, the word "master" means "teacher" or "instructor." Jesus is warning the would-be follower that it will not be easy.

Did you see the film, "Sister Act?" The closing scene involved the jazzed-up choir singing the sedate version of the song, "I Will Follow Him," followed by the souped-up version. Both were powerful renditions. But it's a lot easier to sing than to follow.

We cannot expect an easier time of it than Jesus himself had. But, once having met Jesus, it is difficult to imagine not following wherever he goes.

"And as he sat at dinner in the house, many tax collectors and sinners came and were sitting with him and his disciples. When the Pharisees saw this, they said to his disciples, 'Why does your teacher eat with tax collectors and sinners?' But when he heard this, he replied, 'Those who are well have no need of a physician, but those who are sick. Go and learn what this means, I desire mercy, not sacrifice.' For I have come to call not the righteous but sinners (Matthew 9, 10-13 NRSV).

Jesus is portrayed in the above passage not only as master and teacher but also as the compassionate and wise "doctor" or physician.

The tax-collectors, who were the outcasts of their day, and other sinners were all people who recognized their need of Jesus. They wanted to be with him. They were drawn to him. Instinctively they understood that he could help them and heal them. The Pharisees, so sure of their own righteousness, could not see their own need. This is why the great saints always truly believed themselves great sinners. The closer we draw to Jesus, the more and more aware we are of our own sin. This is not cause for sadness, but for rejoicing. Focusing on Jesus brings joy. Focusing on themselves, on keeping their human-made rules, brought the Pharisees nothing but spiritual blindness.

"A disciple is not above the teacher, nor a slave above the master; it is enough for the disciple to be like the teacher, and the slave like the master (Matthew 10, 24, 25 NRSV)."

This warning is in the midst of Jesus' instructions to his close followers. He wants them to be aware that following him will involve suffering.

" '... whoever does not take up the cross and follow me is not worthy of me. Those who find their life will lose it, and those who lose their life for my sake will find it (Matthew 10, 38-39 NSRV).' "

"Then some of the scribes and Pharisees spoke up, 'Master,' they said, 'we should like to see a sign from you. He replied, 'It is an evil and unfaithful generation that asks for a sign! The only sign it will be given is the sign of the prophet Jonah. For as Jonah remained in the belly of the sea-monster for three days and three nights, so will the Son of man be in the heart of the earth for three days and three nights (Matthew 12, 38-40).' "

Jesus is foretelling the ultimate vindication, his resurrection, in this passage. It is both sad and ironic that the Pharisees call Jesus "Master" and "Teacher," since they despise both him and his message, and have no intention of following him. He said, "Blessed ... are those who hear the word of God and keep it!" (Luke 11, 28) The Pharisees heard Jesus' words over and over, but had no intention of keeping those words.

Jesus is always the master of circumstances. Every Jewish male was expected to pay a half-shekel tax each year for the maintenance of the Temple.

"When they reached Capernaum, the collectors of the temple tax came to Peter and said, 'Does your teacher not pay the temple tax?' He said, 'Yes, he does.' And when he came home, Jesus spoke of it first, asking, 'What do you think, Simon? From whom do kings of the earth take toll or tribute? From their children or from others?' When

Peter said, 'From others,' Jesus said to him, 'Then the children are free. However, so that we do not give offense to them, go to the sea and cast a hook; take the first fish that comes up; and when you open its mouth, you will find a coin; take that and give it to them for you and me (Matthew 17, 24-27 NRSV).' "

"And now a man came to him and said, 'Master, what good deed must I do to possess eternal life?' Jesus said to him, 'Why do you ask me about what is good?' There is one alone who is good. But if you wish to enter into life, keep the commandments.' He said, 'Which ones?' Jesus replied, 'These: You shall not kill. You shall not commit adultery. You shall not steal. You shall not give false witness. Honour you father and your mother. You shall love your neighbor as yourself.' The young man said to him, 'I have kept all these. What more do I need to do?' Jesus said, 'If you wish to be perfect, go and sell your possessions and give the money to the poor, and you will have treasure in heaven; then come, follow me.' But when the young man heard these words he went away sad, for he was a man of great wealth (Matthew 19, 16-22)."

Jesus has penetrating insight into the human psyche. He knew the one thing which this man loved above all others, namely money. With another aspiring disciple, it might be something else. Whatever "it" is, it is worth nothing compared to the honor and privilege of following Jesus.

As St. Paul said, "Yet whatever gains I had, these I have come to regard as loss because of Christ. More than that, I regard everything as loss because of the surpassing value of knowing Christ Jesus my Lord. For his sake I have suffered the loss of all things, and I regard them as rubbish, in order that I may gain Christ and be found in him, not having a righteousness of my own that comes from the law, but one that comes through faith in Christ, the righteousness from God based on faith. I want to know Christ and the power of his resurrection and the sharing of his sufferings by becoming like him in his death, if somehow I may attain the resurrection from the dead (Philippians 3, 7-11 NRSV)."

"Then the Pharisees went away to work out how to trap him in what he said. And they sent their disciples to him, together with some Herodians, to say, 'Master, we know that you are an honest man and teach the way of God in all honesty, and that you are not afraid of anyone, because human rank means nothing to you. Give us your opinion, then. Is is permissible to pay taxes to Caesar or not?' But Jesus was aware of their malice and replied, 'You hypocrites! Why are you putting me to the test? Show me the money you pay the tax with.' They handed him a denarius, and he said, 'Whose portrait is this? Whose title? They replied, 'Caesar's.' Then he said to them, 'Very well, pay Caesar what belongs to

Caesar -- and God what belong to God.' When they heard this they were amazed; they left him alone and went away (Matthew 22, 15-22).' "

If we follow Jesus as our Lord, we need never worry about those who have malice towards us. Jesus will always give to us the wisdom we need in your dealings with such people.

The Pharisees kept trying and trying to trap Jesus with their cleverly-devised questions, to no avail. The Sadducees, who did not believe in the resurrection of the dead, also tried to trap him.

He said to them, "And as for the resurrection of the dead, have you not read what was said to you by God, 'I am the God of Abraham, the God of Isaac, and the God of Jacob'? He is God not of the dead, but of the living (Matthew 22, 31-32 NRSV)."

So much for the Sadducees!

"When the Pharisees heard that he [Jesus] had silenced the Sadducees, they gathered together, and one of them, a lawyer, asked him a question to test him. 'Teacher, which commandment in the law is the greatest?' He said to him, 'You shall love the Lord your God with all your heart, and with all your soul, and with all your mind.' This is the greatest and the first commandment. And a second is like it: 'You shall love your neighbor as yourself.' On these two commandments hang all the law and the prophets (Matthew 22, 34-40 NRSV)."

"On the first day of Unleavened Bread the disciples came to Jesus, saying, 'Where do you want us to make the preparations for you to eat the Passover?' He said, "Go into the city to a certain man, and say to him, 'The Teacher says, My time is near: I will keep the Passover at your house with my disciples.' So the disciples did as Jesus had directed them, and they prepared the Passover meal (Matthew 26, 17-19 NRSV)."

The Gospel of Mark has been called the "straightaway" Gospel because there is such a directness and succinctness about it. There is a great emphasis is on the actions of Jesus.

One evening, Jesus told his disciples, " 'On that day, when evening had come, he said to them, 'Let us go across to the other side.' And leaving the crowd behind, they took him with them in the boat, just as he was. Other boats were with him. A great windstorm arose, and the waves beat into the boat, so that the boat was already being swamped. But he was in the stern, asleep on the cushion; and they woke him up and said to him, 'Teacher, do you not care that we are perishing?' He woke up and rebuked the wind, and said to the sea, 'Peace! Be still!' Then the wind ceased, and there was a dead calm. He said to them, 'Why are you afraid? Have you still no faith?' And they were filled with great awe and said to one another, 'Who is this, that even the wind and the sea obey him (Matthew 4, 35-41 NRSV).'"

The Lord has done great things for me. Still, because of old hurts and old disappointments, sometimes it is sometimes still hard for me to relax and to trust. The Lord understands this, but he still asks us to focus on him. If he can calm the storm on the sea of Galilee, he can calm the storms in our lives, until, at the last, we are safely at harbor, at home, in heaven with him.

While we are still in this life, however, wherever Jesus is, IS home. He not only gives peace, "he IS our peace." (Ephesians 2, 14)

The fifth chapter of Mark's Gospel contains three electrifying accounts of Jesus ministering to people in need. He commands unclean spirits to come out a man, he heals a woman who had spent all her money seeking help (to no avail) from the medical profession, and he raises a dead child to life. This child was the daughter of the president of the synagogue. The distraught father came to Jesus, even though it was probably not "politically correct." As you recall, the religious leaders of the day had difficulty, to put it mildly, accepting Jesus. The father put all such scruples aside. He knew that Jesus could help! Jesus agreed to go with him, but on the way, messengers arrived, saying that the little girl had died.

They said, " 'Your daughter is dead. Why trouble the teacher any further?' But overhearing what they said, Jesus said to the leader of the synagogue, 'Do not fear, only believe.' He allowed no one to follow him except Peter, James, and John, the brother of James. When they came to the house of the leader of the synagogue, he saw a commotion, people weeping and wailing loudly. When he had entered, he said to them, 'Why do you make a commotion and weep? The child is not dead but sleeping.' And they laughed at him. Then he put them all outside, and took the child's father and mother and those who were with him, and went in where the child was. He took her by the hand and said to her, 'Talitha cum,' which means, 'Little girl, get up!' And immediately the girl got up and began to walk about (she was twelve years of age). At this they were overcome with amazement. He strictly ordered them that no one should know this, and told them to give her something to eat (Mark 5, 35b-43 NRSV)."

This account of the raising of the little girl shows Jesus as "master" of the situation from start to finish. The messengers came to say that the little girl was dead and that there was no hope. Jesus refused to accept this. Where Jesus is, there is always hope!

There is no situation where he cannot enter and demonstrate his power. He was laughed at and disregarded, but this did not deter him from his mission. He took with him the child's parents and his disciples and proceeded to speak the word of power.

He deliberately did not take with him those who scorned and mocked. At that time, and now, Jesus has the last word and his word brings life and is life. He is the master of all circumstances.

"James and John, the sons of Zebedee, came forward to him and said to him, 'Teacher, we want you to do for us whatever we ask of you.' And he said to them, What is it you want me to do for you?" And they said to him, 'Grant us to sit, one at your right hand and one at your left, in your glory.' But Jesus said to them, 'You do not know what you are asking. Are you able to drink the cup that I drink, or to be baptized with the baptism that I am baptized with?' They replied, 'We are able.' Then Jesus said to them, 'The cup that I drink you will drink; and with the baptism with which I am baptized, you will be baptized; but to sit at my right hand or at my left is not mine to grant, but it is for those for whom it has been prepared.' When the ten heard this, they began to be angry with James and John. So Jesus called them and said to them, 'You know that among the Gentiles those whom they recognize as their rulers lord it over them, and their great ones are tyrants over them. But it is not so among you; but whoever wishes to become great among you must be your servant, and whoever wishes to be first among you must be slave of all. For the Son of Man came not to be served but to serve, and to give his life a ransom for many (Mark 10,35-45 NRSV).'"

Jesus, although he is Lord and Master, emphasizes, by his own life, that the truly great ones are the truly humble ones, those ready to lay down their lives in service to others.

We think of Mother Teresa in our own time. Can you imagine her flaunting her authority and ordering people around? No. Those who were in the presence of this physically tiny but spiritually giant of a woman were aware of her great joy and her great humility. She was to us an example of a great one being servant of all, even to the poorest of the poor.

WE are the poorest of the poor. We are poor in love. Let us, with Mother Teresa, submit to the lordship of Jesus. Let us acknowledge him as "master" of our lives and let him use us as he will.

"As he came out of the temple, one of his disciples said to him, 'Look, Teacher, what large stones and what large buildings!' Then Jesus asked him, 'Do you see these great buildings? Not one stone will be left here upon another; all will be thrown down (Mark 13, 1-2 NRSV).' "

Jesus began to talk with his followers about the destruction of Jerusalem, persecution of believers, and his own return. Rather than dwelling on when these things will occur, he tells his disciples, " 'But about that day or hour no one knows, neither the angels in heaven, nor the Son, but only the Father. Beware, keep alert; for you do not know when the time will come. It is like a man going on a journey, when he leaves home and puts his slaves in charge, each with his work, and commands the doorkeeper to be on the watch. Therefore, keep awake -- for you do not know when the master of the house will come, in the evening, or at midnight, or at cockcrow, or at dawn, or else he may find you asleep when he comes suddenly. And what I say to you I say to all: Keep awake (Mark 13, 32-37 NRSV).' "

There is a difference in mentally acknowledging Jesus as Lord and Master and acknowledging this on a very deep personal level. Simon Peter experienced this. Jesus got into Peter's fishing boat and taught the crowds from the boat. A floating pulpit!

"When he had finished speaking, he said to Simon, 'Put out into the deep water and let down your nets for a catch.' Simon answered, 'Master, we have worked all night long but have caught nothing. Yet if you say so, I will let down the nets.' When they had done this, they caught so many fish that their nets were beginning to break. So they signaled their partners in the other boat to come and help them, And they came and filled both boats, so that they began to sink. But when Simon Peter saw it, he fell down at Jesus' knees, saying, 'Go away from me, Lord, for I am a sinful man!' For he and all who were with him were amazed at the catch of fish that they had taken; and so also were James and John, sons of Zebedee, who were partners with Simon. Then Jesus said to Simon, 'Do not be afraid; from now on you will be catching people.' When they had brought their boats to shore, they left everything and followed him (Luke 5, 4-11 NRSV)."

Peter had a piercing realization, not only of the power of Christ, but also of his holiness. That is why he knelt before Jesus. Later in Luke's Gospel, we will see Peter making his profession of faith in which he acknowledges that Jesus is the Messiah, the Christ of God (Luke 9, 20).

Jesus "... took with him Peter and John and James, and went up on the mountain to pray. And while he was praying, the appearance of his face changed, and his clothes became dazzling white. Suddenly they saw two men, Moses and Elijah, talking to him. They appeared in glory and were speaking of his departure, which he was about to accomplish at Jerusalem. Now Peter and his companions were weighed down with sleep; but since they had stayed awake, they saw his glory and the two men who stood with him. Just as they were leaving him, Peter said to Jesus, 'Master, it is good for us to be here; let us make three dwellings, one for you, one for Moses, and one for Elijah' –not knowing what he said. While he was saying this, a cloud came and overshadowed them; and they were terrified as they entered the cloud. Then from the cloud came a voice that said, 'This is my Son, my Chosen; listen to him!' When the voice had spoken, Jesus was found alone. And they kept silent and in those days told no one any of the things they had seen (Luke 9, 28-36 NRSV)."

"On the next day, when they had come down from the mountain, a great crowd met him. Just then a man from the crowd shouted, 'Teacher, I beg you to look at my son; he is my only child. Suddenly a spirit seizes him, and all at once he shrieks. It convulses him until he foams at the mouth; it mauls him and will scarcely leave him. I begged your disciples to cast it out, but they could not.' Jesus answered, 'You faithless and perverse generation, how much longer must I be with you and bear with you? Bring your son here.' While he was coming, the demon dashed him to the ground in convulsions. But Jesus rebuked the unclean spirit, healed the boy, and gave him back to his father. And all were astounded at the greatness of God (Luke 9, 37-43a NRSV)."

In the two passages above, Jesus is called "master" by his disciple, Peter, and by an unknown man, desperate to secure help for his son. The lordship of Jesus is demonstrated in remarkable ways, in both cases. In the first case, the Transfiguration, the nature and the authority of Jesus are being validated by God the Father. The outworking of that authority is demonstrated when Jesus and his disciples come down from the mountain. In even the most difficult and distressing cases, such as that of the boy, Jesus still has final authority.

"Just then a lawyer stood up to test Jesus. 'Teacher,' he said, 'what must I do to inherit eternal life?' He said to him, 'What is written in the law? What do you read there?' He answered, 'You shall love the Lord you God with all your heart, and with all your soul, and with all your strength, and with all your mind; and your neighbor as yourself.' And he said to him, 'You have given the right answer; do this, and you will live (Luke 10, 25-28 NRSV)." This lawyer addressed Jesus as an esteemed instructor, indeed a doctor.

Jesus confronted the Pharisees for their hypocrisy

" 'You Pharisees, you clean the outside of the cup and plate, while inside you are filled with extortion and wickedness. Fools (Luke 11, 39-40a)!"

"One of the lawyers answered him, 'Teacher, when you say these things, you insult us too.' And he said, 'Woe also to you lawyers! For you load people with burdens hard to bear, and you yourselves do not lift a finger to ease them (Luke 11,45-46 NRSV).'"

It is interesting that the lawyers, the "experts," called Jesus "master," but they had no corresponding commitment to follow and obey him.

Jesus said, "'Not everyone who says to me, 'Lord, Lord,' will enter the kingdom of heaven, but only the one who does the will of my Father in heaven. On that day many will say to me, 'Lord, Lord, did we not prophesy in your name, and cast out demons in your name, and do many deeds of power in your name?' Then I will declare to them, 'I never knew you; go away from me, you evildoers (Matthew 7, 21-23 NRSV).'"

In the time of Jesus, the lepers were the outcasts. They had a visible, terrible, skin disorder. They were shunned and avoided. "On the way to Jerusalem he (Jesus) was passing along between Samaria and Galilee. And as he entered a village, he was met by ten lepers, who stood at a distance and lifted up their voices and said, 'Jesus, Master, have mercy on us.' When he saw them he said to them, 'Go and show yourselves to the priests.' And as they went they were cleansed. Then one of them, when he saw that he was healed, turned back, praising God with a loud voice; and he fell on his face at Jesus' feet, giving him thanks. Now he was a Samaritan. Then said Jesus, 'Were not ten cleansed? Where are the other nine? Was no one found to return and give praise to God except this foreigner?' And he said to him, 'Rise and go your way; your faith has made you well (Luke 17, 11-19).'"

The lepers knew they were sick. Leprosy has been compared to sin. In our case, we can be very sick inside with sin and its effects, but look perfectly well on the outside.

Jesus waits for us to come to him, to acknowledge both his love for us and his power and authority over us. Can we fall at his feet and call him Lord and Master? Are we aware enough of our need for healing and cleansing to ask him to have mercy on us? The word "mercy" carries with it the meaning of tenderness and compassion. Jesus longs to show forth his tender mercy.

The message of Jesus cannot be silenced. When Jesus entered Jerusalem prior to his death and resurrection, "the whole group of disciples joyfully began to praise God at the top of their voices for all the miracles they had seen. They cried out:

'Blessed is he who is coming
as King in the name of the Lord!
Peace in heaven
and glory in the highest heavens!'

Some Pharisees in the crowd said to him, 'Master, reprove your disciples,' but he answered, 'I tell you, if these keep silence, the stones will cry out (Luke 19, 38-40).' "

We have seen, over and over, how the religious leaders, so sure of their own righteousness, tried to trap Jesus. They could never succeed.

Luke's Gospel tells also, as did the Gospels of Matthew and Mark, about the question of paying taxes to the government. Jesus had just finished telling a parable, the parable of the wicked tenants.

"So they watched him and sent spies who pretended to be honest, in order to trap him by what he said, so as to hand him over to the jurisdiction and authority of the governor. So they asked him, 'Teacher, we know that you are right in what you say and teach, and you show deference to no one, but teach the way of God in accordance with truth. Is it lawful for us to the emperor, or not?' But he perceived their craftiness and said to them, 'Show me a denarius. Whose head and whose title does it bear?' They said, 'The emperor's.' He said to them, 'Then give to the emperor the things that are the emperor's, and to God the things that are God's.' And they were not able in the presence of the people to trap him by what he said; and being amazed by his answer, they became silent (Luke 20, 20-26 NRSV)."

Jesus is Lord and Master of life and death. In the matter of the death of one of his good friends, Lazarus, this lordship is seen in a dramatic way. Lazarus' two sisters were Mary, the quiet, contemplative one, and Martha, the robust, active one.

"When Martha heard that Jesus was coming, she went and met him, while Mary stayed at home. Martha said to Jesus, Lord, if you had been here, my brother would not have died. But even now I know that God will give you whatever you ask of him.' Jesus said to her, 'Your brother will rise again.' Martha said to him, 'I know that he will rise again in the resurrection on the last day.' Jesus said to her, 'I am the resurrection and the life. Those who believe in me, even though they die, will live, and everyone who lives and believes in me will never die. Do you believe this?' She said to him, Yes, Lord, I believe that you are the Messiah, the Son of God, the one coming into the world.' When she had said this, she went back and called her sister Mary, and told her privately, 'The Teacher is here and is calling for you.' And when she heard it, she got up quickly and went to him (John 11, 20-29 NRSV)."

In the presence of Mary and Martha and others, Jesus wept and summoned Lazarus back to life (John, 35-44).

"Now before the festival of the Passover, Jesus knew that his time had come to depart from this world and go to the Father. Having loved his own who were in the world, he loved them to the end. And during supper Jesus, knowing that the Father had given all things into his hands, and that he had come from God and was going to God, got up from the table, took off his outer robe, and tied a towel around himself. Then he poured water into a basin and began to wash the disciples' feet and to wipe them with the towel that was tied around him. After he had washed their feet, had put on his robe, and returned to the table, he said to them, 'Do you know what I have done to you? You call me Teacher and Lord – and you are right. So if I, your Lord and Teacher, have washed your feet, you also ought to wash one another's feet. For I have set you an example, that you also should do as I have done to you (John 13, 1,3-5, 12-15 NRSV).'"

Jesus, by his example, defines leadership. "If any one would be first, he must be last of all and servant of all." (Mark 9, 35) His only "vestment" was a towel wrapped round his waist to wash the feet of his disciples.

After Jesus' death and burial, Mary Magdalene went to his tomb, observed that the stone was no longer there, then ran to Peter and the other disciple to tell them. The disciples came to the tomb and then returned home.

"But Mary stood weeping outside the tomb. As she wept, she bent over to look into the tomb; and she saw two angels in white, sitting where the body of Jesus had been lying, one at the head and the other at the feet. They said to her, 'Woman, why are you weeping?' She said to them, 'They have taken away my Lord, and I do not know where they have laid him.' When she had said this, she turned around and saw Jesus standing there, but she did not know that it was Jesus. Jesus said to her, Woman, why are you weeping? Whom are you looking for?' Supposing him to be the gardener, she said to him, 'Sir, if you have carried him away, tell me where you have laid him, and I will take him away.' Jesus said to her, 'Mary!' She turned and said to him in Hebrew, Rabbouni!' which means Teacher). Jesus said to her, 'Do not hold onto me, because I have not yet ascended to the Father. But go to my brothers and say to them, 'I am ascending to my Father and your Father, to my God and your God.' And Mary Magdalene went and announced to the disciples, 'I have seen the Lord'; and she told them that he had said these things to her (John 20, 11-18 NRSV)."

"Render service with enthusiasm, as to the Lord and not to men and women, knowing that whatever good we do, we will receive the same again from the Lord, whether we are slaves or free. And masters, do the same to them. Stop threatening them, for you know that both of you have the same Master in heaven, and with him there is no partiality (Ephesians 6, 7-9 NRSV)."

"Masters, treat your slaves justly and fairly ,for you know that you also have a Master in heaven." (Colossians 4, 1,NRSV)

It is uncomfortable to read this "master-slave" terminology. Even using the words "employer-employee" still doesn't help much. We are still often like children who say, "When I grow up, no one is going to tell me what to do!" Then we grow up and realize that we are always accountable to someone. Even those in high office are accountable both to God and to those who honored them with such responsibility.

MORNING STAR

"And all the churches shall know that I am the one who searches minds and hearts, and I will give to each of you as your works deserve (Revelation 2, 23b, NRSV)."

"To everyone who conquers and continues to do my works to the end, I will give authority over the nations; to rule them with an iron rod, as when clay pots are shattered – even as I also received authority from my Father. To the one who conquers I will also give the morning star (Revelation 2, 26-28 NRSV)."

The Morning Star is Jesus! This is made clear in the last chapter of the Revelation of St. John. " 'It is I, Jesus, who sent my angel to you with this testimony for the churches. I am the root and the descendant of David, the bright morning star (Revelation 22, 16 NRSV).' "

MOST HIGH

God is sometimes referred to as the "Most High," the One with supreme authority.

"When Abram returned from defeating Chedor-Laomer and the kings who had been on his side, the king of Sodom came to meet him in the valley of Shaveh (that is, the Valley of the King). Melchizedek king of Salem brought bread and wine; he was a priest of God Most High. He pronounced this blessing:

> Blessed be Abram by God Most High,
> Creator of heaven and earth.
> And blessed be God Most High
> for putting your enemies into your clutches (Genesis 14, 17-19)."

There are many references in the Psalms to the Lord as the "Most High."

> "I will give to the LORD the thanks
> due to his righteousness,
> and I will sing praise to the name
> of the LORD, the Most High (Psalm 7, 17)."

> "There is a river whose streams make
> glad the city of God,
> the holy habitation of the Most High (Psalm 46, 4)."

> "Offer to God a sacrifice of
> thanksgiving,
> and pay your vows to
> the Most High;
> and call upon me in the
> day of trouble;
> I will deliver you, and
> you shall glorify me (Psalm 50, 14-15)."

> "I cry to God Most High
> to God who fulfills his purpose for
> me.
> He will send from heaven and save
> me,
> he will put to shame those who
> trample upon me.
> God will send forth his steadfast
> love and his faithfulness (Psalm 57, 2-3)!"

"You who live in the shelter of the Most High, who abide in the shadow of the Almighty, will say to the LORD, 'My refuge and my fortress; my God, in whom I trust (Psalm 91, 1-2 NRSV)."

A very solemn warning against trifling with the sovereignty of God is given in the book of Daniel. "All this came upon King Nebuchadnezzar. At the end of twelve months he was walking on the roof of the royal palace of Babylon, and the king said, 'Is this not magnificent Babylon, which I have built as a royal capital by my mighty power and for my glorious majesty?' While the words were still in the king's mouth, a voice came from heaven: 'O King Nebuchadnezzar, to you it is declared: The kingdom has departed from you! You shall be driven away from human society, and your dwelling shall be with the animals of the field. You shall be made to eat grass like oxen, and seven times shall pass over you, until you have learned that the Most High has sovereignty over the kingdom of mortals and gives it to whom he will. Immediately the sentence was fulfilled against Nebuchadnezzar. He was driven away from human society, ate grass like oxen, and his body was bathed like the dew of heaven, until his hair grew as long as eagles' feathers and his nails became like birds' claws. When that period was over, I, Nebuchadnezzar, lifted my eyes to heaven, and my reason returned to me. I blessed the Most High, and praised and honored the one who lives forever. For his sovereignty is an everlasting sovereignty, and his kingdom endures from generation to generation. All the inhabitants of the earth are accounted as nothing, and he does what he wills with the host of heaven and the inhabitants of the earth. There is no one who can stay his hand or say to him, "What are you doing?' At that time my reason returned to me; and my majesty and splendor were restored to me for the glory of my kingdom. My counselors and my LORDS sought me out, I was reestablished over my kingdom, and still more greatness was added to me. Now I, Nebuchadnezzar, praise and extol and honor the King of heaven, for all his works are truth, and his ways are justice; and he is able to bring low those who walk in pride (Daniel 4, 28-36 NRSV)."

The powers of darkness know the true identity of Jesus, that He is the Son of the Most High God. In the Gospel of Mark, we read about the Gerasene demoniac. Jesus and his disciples had just crossed the sea to the Gerasene country. "And when he had stepped out of the boat, immediately a man out of the tombs with an unclean spirit met him. He lived among the tombs; and no one could restrain him any more, even with a chain; for he had often been restrained with shackles and chains, but the chains he wrenched apart, and the shackles he broke in pieces; and no one had the strength to subdue him. Night and day among the tombs and on the mountains he was always howling and bruising himself with stones. When he saw Jesus from a distance, he ran and bowed down before him; and he shouted at the top of his voice, 'What have you to do with me, Jesus, Son of the Most High God? I adjure you by God, do not torment me.' Then Jesus asked him, 'What is your name?' He replied, 'My name is Legion; for we are many.' He begged him earnestly not to send them out of the country. Now there on the hillside a great herd of swine was feeding; and the unclean spirits begged him, 'Send us into the swine; let us enter them.' So he gave them permission. And the unclean spirits came out and entered the swine, and the herd, numbering about two thousand, rushed down the steep bank into the sea, and were drowned in the sea (Mark 5, 2-13, NRSV)."

The evil spirits knew who Jesus was! They knew He had ultimate authority! Jesus cast the evil spirits out of the man, thus setting him free.

> "... the Most High does not dwell in houses made by
> hands; as the prophet says,'Heaven is my throne,
>   and earth my footstool.
> What house will you build for me,
>   says the Lord,
> or what is the place of my rest?
> Did not my hand make all these
>   things (Acts 7, 48-50)?' "

As we saw in the case of the Gerasene demoniac, evil spirits recognize the identity of Jesus. Paul and Silas were in Philippi and were being pestered by a slave-girl who followed them everywhere. As Luke, tells the story, "As we were going to the place of prayer, we were met by a slave girl who had a spirit of divination and brought her owners much gain by soothsaying. She followed Paul and us, saying, 'These men are servants of the Most High god, who proclaim the way of salvation.' And this she did for many days. But Paul was annoyed, and turned and said to the spirit, 'I charge you in the name of Jesus Christ to come out of her.' And it came out that very hour (Acts 16, 16-18)."

Remember that God is Most High. He is simultaneously with us in our struggles and above us. He has the perspective we lack. Because He is God, He can see the total picture and deliver us out of our troubles in the way that is best for us.

(MOTHER)

This name is in parentheses because God is not directly called "Mother" in the canon of the Scripture. There are, however, verses in which God is compared to a mother.

> "Like an eagle that stirs up its nest,
>   that flutters over its young,
>   spreading out its wings, catching them,
>   bearing them on its pinions ... (Deuteronomy 32, 11)."

This is exactly what a mother eagle does when she is teaching her young eagles to leave the nest and to fly.

> "As a mother comforts her child,
> so I will comfort you;
> you shall be comforted in Jerusalem (Isaiah 66, 13 NRSV)."

Jesus laments over Jerusalem. "O Jerusalem, Jerusalem, killing the prophets and stoning those who are sent to you! How often would I have gathered your children together as a hen gathers her brood under her wings, and you would not (Matthew 23, 37)!' "

OFFSPRING OF DAVID

"I, Jesus, have sent my angel to you with this testimony for the churches. I am the root and the offspring of David, the bright morning star (Revelation 22, 16)."

The first words of the New Testament are "The book of the genealogy of Jesus Christ, the son of David, the son of Abraham" (Matthew 1, 1) followed by a long list of ancestors! All four Gospels refer to his kinship to David. Those in need of healing cry out to him, "Have mercy on us, Son of David (Matthew 9, 27)."

On one occasion, Jesus asked the Pharisees, " 'What do you think of the Christ? Whose son is he?' They said to him, 'The Son of David.' He said to them, 'How is it then that David, inspired by the Spirit, calls him Lord, saying,

> 'The LORD said to my Lord,
> Sit at my right hand,
> til I put thy enemies
> under thy feet?'

If David thus calls him Lord, how is he his son? And no one was able to answer him a word, nor from that day did any one dare ask him any more questions (Matthew 22, 42-45)."

POWER

Jesus was brought before the high priests who were eager to find a way to put him to death. False witness gave conflicting testimonies. Jesus remained silent. The high priest asked, " 'Are you the Christ, the Son of the Blessed?' And Jesus said, 'I am; and you will see the Son of man seated at the right hand of Power, and coming with the clouds of heaven (Mark 14, 61-62).' "

We usually think of power, especially ultimate power, as an attribute of God, not as a name. In this case, the writer of the Gospel is using the terms Blessed and Power as substitutes for the holy name of God, which the Jewish people, out of reverence, would not pronounce.

PRIEST

The first mention in the Bible of a priest is in the book of Genesis. Abram, later to be called Abraham, was returning victorious in battle.

"And Melchizedek king of Salem brought out bread and wine; he was priest of God Most High. And he blessed him and said,

'Blessed be Abram by God Most High,
maker of heaven and earth;
and blessed be God Most High,
who has delivered your enemies
into your hand!'

And Abram gave him a tenth of everything." (Genesis 14, 18-20)

We are to hear of the mysterious Melchisedek later, in the Psalms and in letter to the Hebrews.

Psalm 110 is a psalm of David, a royal psalm, in honor of the Messiah who is to come:

"The LORD has sworn
and will not change his mind,
'You are a priest for ever
according to the order of Melchizedek (Psalm 110, 4 NRSV)."

We'll return to Melchizedek later, but let's look now at the whole idea of the priesthood in the Old Testament or the Hebrew Scriptures. In the book of Exodus, we find God saying to Moses,

"Then bring near to you Aaron your brother,
and his sons with him, from among the people of Israel,
to serve me as priests -- Aaron and Aaron's sons,
Nadab and Abihu, Eleazer and Ithamar. And you shall make
holy garments for Aaron your brother,
for glory and for beauty (Exodus 28, 1-2)."

It is clear that the first duty of the priest is to serve GOD. The book of Exodus goes into fascinating detail about the meaning of the priestly vestments and about the ordination service (Exodus 28, 29). The priest is anointed with oil and touched upon the ears, hands, and feet with the blood of the sacrificial ram to indicated the consecration of the entire person for God's service.

The focus of our attention is on Jesus as our own Priest, our mediator.

"For there is one God; there is also one mediator between God and humankind, Christ Jesus, himself human, who gave himself a ransom for all (1 Timothy 2, 5-6a, NRSV)."

The Letter to the Hebrews offers many insights into the priesthood of Jesus.

"Since therefore the children share in flesh and blood, he himself likewise partook of the same nature, that through death he might destroy him who has the power of death, that is, the devil, and deliver all those who through fear of death were subject to lifelong bondage. For surely it is not with angels that he is concerned but with the descendants of Abraham. Therefore he had to be made like his brethren in every respect so that he might become a merciful and faithful high priest in the service of God, to make expiation for the sins of the people. For because he himself has suffered and been tempted, he is able to help those who are tempted (Hebrews 2, 14-18)."

"Therefore, holy brethren, who share in a heavenly call, consider Jesus, the apostle and high priest of our confession. He was faithful to him who appointed him ... (Hebrews 3, 1-2a)."

The Greek word for "consider" is "katanoeo." This means to observe fully, to behold, to discover, and to perceive. To discover implies that there has been a diligent search.

Is God an elective (God 101) or is God our everything, our passion, the very reason for our existence?

"You will seek me and find me; when you seek me
    with all your heart,
I will be found by you, says the LORD ... (Jeremiah 29, 13,14a)."

"Since then we have a great high priest who has passed through the heavens, Jesus, the Son of God, let us hold fast our confession. For we have not a high priest who is unable to sympathize with our weaknesses, but one who in every respect has been tempted as we are, yet without sin. Let us then with confidence draw near to the throne of grace, that we may receive mercy and find grace to help in time of need." (Hebrews 4, 14-16)

"Every high priest chosen from among mortals is put in charge of things pertaining to God on their behalf, to offer gifts and sacrifices for sins. He is able to deal gently with the ignorant and wayward, since he himself is subject to weakness; and because of this he must offer sacrifice for his own sins as well as for those of the people. And one does not presume to take this honor, but takes it only when called by God, just as Aaron was.

So also Christ did not glorify himself in becoming a high priest, but was appointed by the one who said to him,

'You are my Son,
today I have begotten you';
as he says also in another place,
'You are a priest forever,
according to the order of Melchizedek.'

In the days of his flesh, Jesus offered up prayers and supplications, with loud cries and tears, to the one who was able to save him from death, and he was heard because of his reverent submission. Although he was a Son, he learned obedience through what he suffered; and having been made perfect, he became the source of eternal salvation for all who obey him, having been designated by God a high priest according to the order of Melchizedek (Hebrews 5, 1-10 NRSV)."

"Human beings, of course, swear by someone greater than themselves, and an oath given as confirmation puts an end to all dispute. In the same way, when God desired to show even more clearly to the heirs of the promise the unchangeable character of his purpose, he guaranteed it by an oath, so that through two unchangeable things, in which it is impossible that God would prove false, we who have taken refuge might be strongly encouraged to seize the hope set before us. We have this hope, a sure and steadfast anchor of the soul, a hope that enters the inner shrine behind the curtain, where Jesus, a forerunner in our behalf, has entered, having become a high priest forever according to the order of Melchizedek (Hebrews 6, 16-20 NRSV)."

"For it was fitting that we should have such a high priest, holy, blameless, unstained, separated from sinners, exalted above the heavens. Unlike the other high priests, he has no need to offer sacrifices day after day first for his own sins, and then for those of the people; this he did once for all when he offered himself. For the law appoints as high priests those who are subject to weakness, but the word of the oath, which came later than the law, appoints a Son who has been made perfect forever (Hebrews 7, 26-28 NRSV)."

"Now the main point in what we are saying is this: We have such a high priest, one who is seated at the right hand of the throne of the Majesty in the heavens, a minister in the sanctuary and the true tent that the LORD, and not any mortal, has set up. For every high priest is appointed to offer gifts and sacrifices; hence it is necessary for this priest also to have something to offer. Now if he were in earth, he would not be a priest at all, since there are priests who offer gifts according to the law. They offer worship in a sanctuary that is a sketch and shadow of the heavenly one; for Moses, when he was about to erect the tent, was warned, 'See that you make everything according to the pattern that was shown you on the mountain.' But Jesus has now obtained a more excellent ministry, and to that degree he is the mediator of a better covenant, which has been enacted through better promises (Hebrews 8, 1-7 NRSV)."

"When Christ appeared as a high priest of the good things that have come, then through the greater and more perfect tent (not made with hands, that is, not of this creation) he entered once for all into the Holy Place, taking not the blood of goats and calves but his own blood, thus securing an eternal redemption. For if the sprinkling of defiled persons with the blood of goats and bulls and with the ashes of a heifer sanctifies for the purification of the flesh, how much more shall the blood of Christ, who through the eternal Spirit offered himself without blemish to God, purify your conscience from dead works to serve the living God (Hebrews 9, 11-14)."

"Indeed, under the law almost everything is purified with blood, and without the shedding of blood there is no forgiveness of sins. Thus it was necessary for the copies of the heavenly things to be purified with these rites, but the heavenly things themselves with better sacrifices than these. For Christ has entered, not into a sanctuary made with hands, a copy of the true one, but into heaven itself, now to appear in the presence of God on our behalf. Nor was it to offer himself repeatedly, as the high priest enters the Holy Place yearly with blood not his own; for then he would have had to suffer repeatedly since the foundation of the world. But as it is, he has appeared once for all at the end of the age to put away sin by the sacrifice of himself (Hebrews 9, 22-26)."

"Therefore, my friends, since we have confidence to enter the sanctuary by the blood of Jesus, by the new and living way that he opened for us through the curtain (that is, through his flesh), and since we have a great priest over the house of God, let us approach with a true heart in full assurance of faith, with our hearts sprinkled clean from an evil conscience and our bodies washed with pure water. Let us hold fast to the confession of our hope without wavering, for he who has promised is faithful (Hebrews 10, 19-23)."

Jesus was the perfect offering, the perfect sacrifice for our sins. Our sacrifice is one of praise. "Through him then let us continually offer up a sacrifice of praise to God, that is, the fruit of our lips that acknowledge his name (Hebrews 13, 15)."

PRINCE

In the book of Isaiah, we learn about the promised child born to be king.

"For to us a child is born,
  to us a son is given;
 and the government will be upon
  his shoulder,
  and his name will be called
'Wonderful Counselor, Mighty God,
  Everlasting Father,
    Prince of Peace (Isaiah 9, 6)."

After the healing of the lame man outside the Beautiful Gate of the Temple, Peter addressed the people,

"… 'You Israelites, why do you wonder at this, or why do you stare at us, as though by our own power or piety we had made him walk? The God of Abraham, the God of Isaac, and the God of Jacob, the God of our ancestors has glorified his servant Jesus, whom you handed over and rejected in the presence of Pilate, though he had decided to release him. But you rejected the Holy and Righteous One and asked to have a murderer given to you, and you killed the Author of life, whom God raised from the dead. To this we are witnesses. And by faith in his name, his name itself has made this man strong, whom you see and know; and the faith that is through Jesus has given him this perfect health in the presence of all of you (Acts 3, 12-16 NRSV)."

PROPHET

Jesus comes into the world not only as One who speaks forth the words of God but who actually IS the Word of God. "In the beginning was the Word, and the Word was with God, and the Word was God (John 1, 1)."

All four Gospels tell that Jesus would be rejected by his own. "He was in the world, and the world was made through him, yet the world knew him not. He came to his own home, and his own people received him not (John 1, 10-11)."

JESUS CHRIST, Son of God and Son of Mary, was rejected. How extraordinary, isn't it, to think of this rejection of Our Lord? How could this be?

The Gospel continues, "But to all who received him, who believed in his name, he gave power to become children of God; who were born, not of blood nor of the will of the flesh nor of the will of man, but of God. And the Word became flesh and dwelt among us, full of grace and truth; we have beheld his glory, glory as of the only Son from the Father (John 1, 12-14)."

Again, all four Gospels speak of this rejection:

Jesus was in his hometown of Nazareth, teaching in the synagogue. The people were "astounded and said, 'Where did this man get this wisdom and these deeds of power? Is this not the carpenter's son? Is not his mother called Mary? And are not his brothers James and Joseph and Simon and Judas? And are not all his sisters with us? Where then did this man get all this?' And they took offense at him. But Jesus said to them, 'A prophet is not without honor except in his own country and in his own house.' And he did not do many mighty works there, because of their unbelief (Matthew 13, 53-58)."

"He went away from there and came to his own country; and his disciples followed him. And on the sabbath he began to teach in the synagogue; and many who heard him were astonished, saying, 'Where did this man get all this? What is the wisdom given to him? What mighty works are wrought by his hands! Is not this the carpenter, the son of Mary and brother of James and Joseph and Judas and Simon, and are not his sisters here with us?' And they took offense at him. And Jesus said to them, 'A prophet is not without honor, except in his own country, and among his own kin, and in his own house.' And he could do no mighty works there, except that he laid his hands upon a few sick people and healed them. And he marveled because of their unbelief (Mark 6, 1-6)."

"And he came to Nazareth, where he had been brought up; and he went to the synagogue, as his custom was, on the sabbath day. And he stood up to read; and there was given to him the book of the prophet

Isaiah. He opened the book and found the place where it was written,

> 'The Spirit of the LORD is upon me,
> because he has anointed me to
> preach good news to the poor
> He has sent me to proclaim release
> to the captives
> and recovering of sight to the blind,
> to set at liberty those who are
> oppressed,
> to proclaim the acceptable year of
> the LORD.'

And he closed the book, and gave it back to the attendant, and sat down; and the eyes of all in the synagogue were fixed on him. And he began to say to them, 'Today this scripture has been fulfilled in your hearing.' And all spoke well of him, and wondered at the gracious words which proceeded out of his mouth; and they said, 'Is not this Joseph's son?' And he said to them, 'Doubtless you will quote to me this proverb, 'Physician, heal yourself; what we heard you did at Capernaum, do here also in your own country.' And he said, 'Truly, I say to you, no prophet is acceptable in his own country. But in truth, I tell you, there were many widows in Israel in the days of Elijah, when the heaven was shut up three years and six months, when there came a great famine over all the land; and Elijah was sent to none of them but only to Zarephath, in the land of Sidon, to a woman who was a widow. And there were many lepers in Israel in the time of the prophet Elisha; and none of them was cleansed, but only Naaman the Syrian.' When they heard this, all in the synagogue were filled with wrath. And they rose up and put him out of the city, and led him to the brow of the hill on which their city was built, that they might throw him down headlong. But passing through the midst of them he went away (Luke 4, 16-30)."

Jesus, after his illuminating conversation with the Samaritan woman ("the woman at the well") spent an additional two days with the Samaritan people. "After the two days he departed to Galilee. For Jesus himself testified that a prophet has no honor in his own country. So when he went to Galilee, the Galileans welcomed him (John 4, 43-45a)."

RABBI

John the Baptist "looked at Jesus as he walked, and said, 'Behold the Lamb of God!' The two disciples heard him say this, and they followed Jesus. Jesus turned, and saw them following, and said to them, 'What do you seek?' And they said to him, 'Rabbi' (which means Teacher), 'where are you staying?' He said to them, 'Come and see (John 1, 36-39a).' "

"The next day Jesus decided to go to Galilee. And he found Philip and said to him, 'Follow me.' Now Philip was from Bethsaida, the city of Andrew and Peter. Philip found Nathanael, and said to him, 'We have found him of whom Moses in the law and also the prophets wrote, Jesus of Nazareth, the son of Joseph.' Nathanael said to him, 'Can anything good come out of Nazareth?' Philip said to him, 'Come and see.' Jesus saw Nathanael coming to him, and said of him, 'Behold, an Israelite indeed, in whom there is no guile!' Nathanael said to him, 'How do you know me?' Jesus answered him, 'Before Philip called you, when you were under the fig tree, I saw you.' Nathanael answered him, 'Rabbi, you are the Son of God! You are the King of Israel!' Jesus answered him, 'Because I said to you, I saw you under the fig tree, do you believe? You shall see greater things than these.' And he said to him, 'Truly, truly, I say to you, you will see heaven opened, and the angels of God ascending and descending upon the Son of man (John 1, 43-51).' "

"Now there was a Pharisee named Nicodemus, a leader of the Jews. He came to Jesus by night and said to him, 'Rabbi, we know that you are a teacher who has come from God; for no one can do these things that you do apart from the presence of God.' Jesus answered him, 'Very truly, I tell you, no one can see the kingdom of God without being born from above.' Nicodemus said to him, 'How can anyone be born after having grown old? Can one enter a second time into the mother's womb and be born?' Jesus answered, 'Very truly, I tell you, no one can enter the kingdom of God without being born of water and Spirit. What is born of the flesh is flesh, and what is born of the Spirit is spirit. Do not be astonished that I said to you, 'You must be born from above.' The wind blows where it chooses, and you hear the sound of it, but you do not know where it comes from or where it goes. So it is with everyone who is born of the Spirit.' Nicodemus said to him, 'How can these things be?' Jesus answered him, 'Are you a teacher of Israel, and yet you do not understand these things? 'Very truly, I tell you, we speak of what we know and testify to what we have seen; yet you do not receive our testimony. If I have told you about earthly things and you do not believe, how can you believe if I tell you about heavenly things? No one has ascended into heaven except the one who descended from heaven, the Son of Man. And just as Moses lifted up the serpent in the wilderness, so must the Son of Man be lifted up, that whoever believes in him may have eternal life. 'For God so loved the world that he gave his only Son, so that everyone who believes in him may not perish but have eternal life. 'Indeed God did not send his Son into the world to condemn the world, but in order that the world might be saved through him (John 3, 1-17 NRSV).' "

REDEEMER

Throughout the Hebrew Scriptures (Old Testament), God is portrayed as the One with ultimate power, more than capable of redeeming his people when others oppress them.

The Lord said to Moses, "... I have heard the groaning of the people of Israel whom the Egyptians hold in bondage and I have remembered my covenant. Say therefore to the people of Israel, 'I am the LORD, and I will bring you out from under the burdens of the Egyptians, and I will deliver you from their bondage, and I will redeem you with an outstretched arm and with great acts of judgment, and I will take you for my people, and I will be your God; and you shall know that I am the LORD your God, who has brought you out from under the burdens of the Egyptians (Exodus 6, 5-7)."

David praises God, saying, "Therefore thou art great, O LORD God; for there is none like thee, and there is no God besides thee, according to all that we have heard with our ears. What other nation on earth is like thy people Israel, whom God went to redeem to be his people, making himself a great name, and doing for them great and terrible things by driving out before his people a nation and its gods (2 Samuel 7, 22-23)?"

Job, in the midst of his suffering and in the midst of the misunderstanding of his so-called friends, declared,

"I know that my Redeemer lives,
  and at last he will stand upon the earth;
  and after my skin has been thus destroyed,
  then from my flesh I shall see God,
  whom I shall see on my side,
  and my eyes shall behold,
  and not another (Job 19, 25-27)."

There are many references in the Psalms to God's redeeming work.

"Let the words of my mouth and the
  meditation of my heart
  be acceptable in thy sight,
  O LORD, my rock and my
  redeemer (Psalm 19, 14)."

The Hebrew root word (gaal) in the above passage carries with it the meaning of avenger, revenger, ransomer, and taking the part of the next of kin. This was the word used in the book of Ruth. Boaz took on the role of the kinsman-redeemer on behalf of Ruth.

> On the Cross, Jesus prayed from Psalm 31, 5:
> "Into thy hands I commit my spirit;
>   thou hast redeemed me, O LORD,
>   faithful God (Psalm 31, 5)."

Psalm 78 tells of the great acts of God on behalf of Israel.

> "They remembered that God was
>   their rock,
>   the Most High God their
>   redeemer (Psalm 78, 35)."

"But now thus says the LORD,
 he who created you, O Jacob,
 he who formed you, O Israel:
 'Fear not, for I have redeemed
    you.
  I have called you by name,
    you are mine.
  When you pass through the waters
    I will be with you;
  and through the rivers,
    they shall not overwhelm you;
  when you walk through fire
    you shall not be burned,
  and the flame shall not consume you (Isaiah 43, 1-2)."

"Thus says the LORD, the King of Israel
  and his Redeemer, the LORD of hosts:
  'I am the first and I am the last;
    besides me there is no god (Isaiah 44, 6)."

"Sing, O heavens, for the LORD has done it;
  shout, O depths of the earth;
  break forth into singing, O mountains,
    O forest, and every tree in it!

  For the LORD has redeemed Jacob,
    and will be glorified in Israel (Isaiah 44, 22)!"

"Thus says the LORD, your Redeemer,

who formed you from the womb:
'I am the LORD, who made all things,
   who stretched out the heavens
     alone,
who spread out the earth … (Isaiah 44, 24)."

"Our Redeemer -- the LORD of hosts is his name --
   is the Holy One of Israel (Isaiah 47, 4)."

"Thus says the LORD, your Redeemer, the Holy One of Israel: I am the LORD, your God, who teaches you for your own good, who leads you in the way you should go (Isaiah 48, 17 NRSV)."

"Thus says the LORD,
   the Redeemer of Israel and his
     Holy One,
to one deeply despised,
abhorred by the nations,
   the servant of rulers:
'Kings shall see and arise;
  princes, and they shall prostrate
     themselves,
because of the LORD, who is faithful,
   the Holy One of Israel, who has
     chosen you (Isaiah 49, 7).' "

"How beautiful upon the
    mountains
are the feet of the messenger
who announces peace, who brings good news,
who announces salvation,
who says to Zion,
  'Your God reigns.'
Listen! Your sentinels lift up their
   voices,
together they sing for joy; for in plain sight they see
   the return of the LORD to Zion.
Break forth into singing,
   you ruins of Jerusalem;
for the LORD has comforted his
   people,
he has redeemed Jerusalem.
The LORD has bared his holy arm
before the eyes of all the
   nations;

and all the ends of the earth shall
see the salvation of our God (Isaiah 52, 7-10 NRSV)."

"Fear not, for you will not be
    ashamed;
be not confounded, for you will
    not be put to shame;
for you will forget the shame of your
    youth,
and the reproach of your
widowhood you will remember
    no more.
For your maker is your husband,
the LORD of hosts is his name;
and the Holy One of Israel is your
    Redeemer,
the God of the whole earth he is
    called (Isaiah 54, 5)."

"Whereas you have been forsaken
and hated,
with no one passing through,
I will make you majestic for ever,
a joy from age to age.
You shall suck the milk of nations,
you shall suck the breasts of kings;
and you shall know that I, the LORD,
    am your Savior
and your Redeemer, the Mighty
One of Jacob (Isaiah 60, 15-16)."

"I will recount the gracious deeds of the LORD, the praiseworthy acts of the LORD, because of all that the LORD has done for us, and the great favor to the house of Israel that he has shown them according to his mercy, according to the abundance of his steadfast love. For he said, 'Surely they are my people, children who will not deal falsely': and he became their savior in all their distress. It was no messenger or angel but his presence that saved them; in his love and in his pity he redeemed them; he lifted them up and carried them all the days of old
(Isaiah 63, 7-9 NRSV).

"For thou art our Father,
    though Abraham does not know
        us
    and Israel does not acknowledge
        us;
    thou, O LORD, art our Father,

> our Redeemer from of old is thy
>   name (Isaiah 63, 16)."

"... the LORD has ransomed
Jacob,
and has redeemed him from
  hands too strong for him (Jeremiah 31, 11)."

" 'Thus says the LORD of hosts:
The people of Israel are oppressed,
and the people of Judah with them;
all who took them captive have held them fast,
they refuse to let them go.
Their Redeemer is strong,
the LORD of hosts is his name.
He will surely plead their cause,
that he may give rest to the earth,
but unrest to the inhabitants of Zion (Jeremiah 50, 33-34)."

We turn now to references in the New Testament about God as Redeemer.

The elderly priest, Zechariah, father of John the Baptist, proclaims the future redemption of God's people:

"Blessed be the LORD God of Israel,
  for he has visited and redeemed his
    people,
  and has raised up a horn of salvation
    for us
  in the house of his servant David,
  as he spoke by the mouth of his
    holy prophets from of old,
  that we should be saved from our
    enemies,
  and from the hand of all who hate us;
  to perform the mercy promised to
    our fathers
  and to remember his holy covenant,
  the oath which he swore to our
  father Abraham, to grant us
  that we, being delivered from the
    hand of our enemies,
  might serve him without fear,
  in holiness and righteousness before
    him all the days of our life.
  And you, child, will be called the

> prophet of the Most High;
> for you will go before the Lord to
> prepare his ways,
> to give knowledge of salvation to
> his people
> in the forgiveness of their sins,
> through the tender mercy of our
> God,
> when the day shall dawn upon us
> from on high
> to give light to those who sit in
> darkness and in the shadow of
> death,
> to guide our feet into the way of
> peace (Luke 1, 68-79).' "

The book of Acts tells us about Jesus' ascension. His mission on this earth was accomplished and it was time to return home to his Father. He told his apostles to stay in Jerusalem until they had received the "promise of the Father," the Holy Spirit.

" 'But you will receive power when the Holy Spirit has come upon you; and you will be my witnesses in Jerusalem, in all Judea and Samaria, and to the ends of the earth.' When he had said this, as they were watching, he was lifted up, and a cloud took him out of their sight. While he was going and they were gazing up toward heaven, suddenly two men in white robes stood by them. They said, 'Men of Galilee, why do you stand looking up toward heaven? This Jesus, who has been taken up into heaven, will come in the same way as you saw him go into heaven (Acts 1, 8-11 NRSV)."

We are told of how Jesus will return. Jesus himself told us how it will be.

" 'There will be signs in the sun, the moon, and the stars, and on the earth distress among nations confused by the roaring of the sea and the waves. People will faint from fear and foreboding of what is coming upon the world, for the powers of heaven will be shaken. Then they will see the Son of Man coming in a cloud with power and great glory. Now when these things begin to take place, stand up and raise your heads, because your redemption is drawing near (Luke 21, 25-28 NRSV).' "

Again, let's look at this concept of redemption.

"But now, apart from the law, the righteousness of God has been disclosed, and is attested by the law and the prophets, the righteousness of God through faith in Jesus Christ for all who believe. For there is no distinction, since all have sinned and fall short of the glory of God; they are now justified by his grace as a gift, through the redemption that is in Christ Jesus, whom God put forward as a sacrifice of atonement by his blood, effective through faith. He did this to show his righteousness, because in his divine forbearance he had passed over the sins previously committed; it was to prove that he himself is righteous and that he justifies the one who has faith in Jesus (Romans 3, 21-26, NRSV)."

We are told that our body, as well as our soul and spirit, will be "redeemed" or set free.

"We know that the whole creation has been groaning in labor pains until now; and not only the creation, but we ourselves, who have the first fruits of the Spirit, groan inwardly while we wait for adoption, the redemption of our bodies. For in hope we were saved. Now hope that is seen is not hope. For who hopes for what is seen? But if we hope for what we do not see, we wait for it with patience (Romans 8, 22-25, NRSV)."

We are brave as we launch out in radical faith and trust to live for the Lord and to wait for the Lord. Our destiny is in our Lord's wise hands.

"Consider your own call, brothers and sisters: not many of you were wise by human standards, not many were powerful, not many were of noble birth. But God chose what is foolish in the world to shame the wise; God chose what is weak in the world to shame the strong; God chose what is low and despised in the world, things that are not, to reduce to nothing things that are, so that no one might boast in the presence of God. He is the source of your life in Christ Jesus, who became for us wisdom from God, and righteousness and sanctification and redemption, in order that, as it is written, 'Let the one who boasts, boast in the Lord (1 Corinthians 1, 26-31 NRSV).'"

"Christ redeemed us from the curse of the law by becoming a curse for us – for it is written, 'Cursed is everyone who hangs on a tree – in order that in Christ Jesus the blessing of Abraham might come to the Gentiles, so that we might receive the promise of the Spirit through faith (Galatians 3, 13-14 NRSV)."

"But when the fullness of time had come, God sent his Son, born of a woman, born under the law, in order to redeem those who were under the law, so that we might receive adoption as children. And because you are children, God has sent the Spirit of his Son into our hearts, crying, 'Abba! Father!' So you are no longer a slave but a child, and if a child then also an heir, through God (Galatians 4, 4-7 NRSV)."

"Blessed be the God and Father of our Lord Jesus Christ, who has blessed us in Christ with every spiritual blessing in the heavenly places, just as he chose us in Christ before the foundation of the world to be holy and blameless before him in love. He destined us for adoption as his children through Jesus Christ, according to the good pleasure of his will, to the praise of his glorious grace that he freely bestowed on us in the Beloved. In him we have redemption thorough his blood, the forgiveness of our trespasses, according to the riches of his grace that he lavished on us. With all wisdom and insight he has made known to us the mystery of his will, according to his good pleasure that he set forth in Christ, as a plan for the fullness of time, to gather up all things in him, things in heaven and things on earth (Ephesians 1, 3-10 NRSV)."

The above verse tells us very clearly what is the will of God. It is to gather up all things -- all things -- both in heaven and on earth in the Lord Jesus Christ. That is God's intent.

"Let no evil talk come out of your mouths, but only such as is good for edifying, as fits the occasion, that it may impart grace to those who hear. And do not grieve the Holy Spirit of God, in whom you were sealed for the day of redemption (Ephesians 4, 29-30)."

"He has delivered us from the dominion of darkness and transferred us to the kingdom of his beloved Son, in whom we have redemption, the forgiveness of sins (Colossians 1, 13-14)."

"But when Christ appeared as a high priest of the good things that have come, then through the greater and more perfect tent (not made with hands, that is, not of this creation) he entered once for all into the Holy Place, taking not the blood of goats and calves but his own blood, thus securing an eternal redemption. For if the sprinkling of defiled persons with the blood of goats and bulls and with the ashes of a heifer sanctifies for the purification of the flesh, how much more shall the blood of Christ, who through the eternal Spirit offered himself without blemish to God, purify your conscience from dead works to serve the living God. Therefore he is the mediator of a new covenant, so that those who are called may receive the promised eternal inheritance, since a death has occurred which redeems them from the transgressions under the first covenant (Hebrews 9, 11-15)."

"You know that you were ransomed from the futile ways inherited from your ancestors, not with perishable things like silver or gold, but with the precious blood of Christ, like that of a lamb without defect or blemish. He was destined before the foundation of the world, but was revealed at the end of the ages for your sake. Through him you have come to trust in God who raised him from the dead and gave him glory, so that your faith and hope are set in God (1 Peter 1, 18-21 NRSV)."

The word translated "ransom" has also been translated "redemption." A celestial hymn, the "Song to the Lamb," is found in the book of the Revelation. Again, the sense of redemption is here, although the more modern translations use the word "ransom" or "bought."

"Then I saw between the throne and the four living creatures and among the elders a Lamb standing as if it had been slaughtered, having seven horns and seven eyes, which are the seven spirits of God sent out into all the earth. He went and took the scroll from the right hand of the one who was seated on the throne. When he had taken the scroll, the four living creatures and twenty-four elders fell before the Lamb, each holding a harp and golden bowls full of incense, which are the prayers of the saints. They sang a new song: 'You are worthy to take the scroll and to open its seals, for you were slaughtered and by your blood you ransomed for God saints from every tribe and language and people and nation; you have made them to be a kingdom and priests serving our God, and they will reign on earth. Then I looked, and I heard the voice of many angels surrounding the throne and the living creatures and the elders; they numbered myriads of myriads and thousands of thousands, singing with full voice, 'Worthy is the Lamb that was slaughtered to receive power and wealth and wisdom and might and honor and glory and blessing!' Then I heard every creature in heaven and on earth and under the earth and in the sea, and all that is in them, singing, 'To the one seated on the throne and to the Lamb be blessing and honor and glory and might forever and ever (Revelation 5, 6-13 NRSV)."

THE ROCK

"The Rock, his work is perfect;
for all his ways are justice.
A God of faithfulness and without
   iniquity,
just and right is he (Deuteronomy 32, 4)."

Faithless Israel was rebuked for being "unmindful of the Rock that begot you (Deuteronomy 32, 18)."

After the birth of her son, Samuel, Hannah rejoiced.

"Hannah also prayed and said,

> 'My heart exults in the LORD;
> my strength is exalted in the LORD.
> My mouth derides my enemies,
> because I rejoice in thy salvation.
>
> There is none holy like the LORD,
> there is none besides thee;
> there is no rock like our God.
> Talk no more so very proudly,
> let not arrogance come from your mouth;
> for the LORD is a God of knowledge,
> and by him actions are weighed (1 Samuel 2, 1-3).' "

"And David spoke to the LORD the words of this song on the day when the LORD delivered him from the hand of all his enemies, and from the hand of Saul. He said,

> 'The LORD is my rock, and my
> fortress, and my deliverer,
> my God, my rock, in whom I
> take refuge,
> my shield and the horn of my
> salvation,
> my stronghold and my refuge,
> my savior... (2 Samuel 22, 1-3).' "

" 'For who is God, but the LORD?
And who is a rock, except our
God?' " (2 Samuel 22, 32)

" 'The LORD lives; and blessed be my
rock,
and exalted be my God, the rock
of my salvation (2 Samuel 22, 47).' "

"Now these are the last words of David:
The oracle of David, the son of
Jesse,
the oracle of the man who was
raised on high,
the anointed of the God of Jacob,
the sweet psalmist of Israel:

'The Spirit of the LORD speaks by
me,
his word is upon my tongue.

> The God of Israel has spoken,
> the Rock of Israel has said to me:
> When one rules justly over men,
> ruling in the fear of God,
> he dawns on them like the morning light,
> like the sun shining forth upon a cloudless morning,
> like rain that makes the grass to sprout from the earth (2 Samuel 23, 1-4).' "

> "I love thee, O LORD, my strength.
> The LORD is my rock, and my fortress and my deliverer,
> my God, my rock, in whom I take refuge,
> my shield, and the horn of my salvation, my stronghold (Psalm 18, 1-2)."

> "In thee, O LORD, do I seek refuge;
> let me never be put to shame;
> in thy righteousness deliver me!
> Incline thy ear to me,
> rescue me speedily!
> Be thou a rock of refuge for me,
> a strong fortress to save me!
>
> Yea, thou art my rock and my fortress;
> for thy name's sake lead me and guide me,
> take me out of the net which is hidden for me,
> for thou art my refuge.
> Into thy hands I commit my spirit;
> for thou hast redeemed me, O LORD, faithful God (Psalm 31, 1-5)."

> "For God alone my soul waits in silence;
> from him comes my salvation.
> He only is my rock and my salvation,
> my fortress; I shall not be greatly moved (Psalm 62, 1-2)."

These are only a few of the Psalms in which we find references to

God as a strong rock.

> "Trust in the LORD for ever,
> for the LORD God
> is an everlasting rock (Isaiah 26, 4)."

"You shall have a song as in the night when a holy feast is kept; and gladness of heart, as when one sets out to the sound of the flute to go to the mountain of the LORD, to the Rock of Israel (Isaiah 30, 29)."

"What then are we to say? Gentiles, who did not strive for righteousness, have attained it, that is, righteousness through faith; but Israel, who did strive for righteousness that is based on the law, did not succeed in fulfilling the law. Why not? Because they did not strive for it on the basis of faith, but as if it were based on works. They have stumbled over the stumbling stone, as it is written, 'See, I am laying in Zion a stone that will make people stumble, a rock that will make them fall, and whoever believes in him will not be put to shame (Romans 9, 30-33 NRSV).'"

"I do not want you to be unaware, brothers and sisters, that our ancestors were all under the cloud, and all passed through the sea, and all were baptized into Moses in the cloud and in the sea, and all ate the same spiritual food, and all drank the same spiritual drink. For they drank from the spiritual rock that followed them, and the rock was Christ (1 Corinthians 10, 1-4 NRSV)."

"Come to him [Jesus], a living stone, though rejected by mortals yet chosen and precious in God's sight, and like living stones, let yourselves be built into a spiritual house, to be a holy priesthood, to offer spiritual sacrifices acceptable to God through Jesus Christ. For it stands in scripture: 'See, I am laying in Zion a stone, a cornerstone chosen and precious; and whoever believes in him will not be put to shame.' To you then who believe, he is precious; but for those who do not believe, 'The stone rejected that the builders rejected has become the very head of the corner,' and 'A stone that makes them stumble, and a rock that makes them fall.' They stumble because they disobey the word, as they were destined to do. But you are a chosen race, a royal priesthood, a holy nation, God's own people, in order that you may proclaim the mighty acts of him who called you out of darkness into his marvelous light (1 Peter 2, 4-9 NRSV)."

ROOT

This is more a descriptive word than an actual name.

"On that day the root of Jesse shall stand as a signal to the peoples; the nation shall inquire of him, and his dwelling shall be glorious (Isaiah 11, 10 NRSV)." This is a reference to the time when Jesus comes as the triumphant King and Messiah.

We turn now to a scene in heaven described in the book of the Revelation. "And I saw in the right hand of him who was seated on the throne a scroll written within and on the back, sealed with seven seals; and I saw a strong angel proclaiming with a loud voice, 'Who is worthy to open the scroll and break its seals?' And no one in heaven or on earth or under the earth was able to open the scroll or to look into it, and I wept much that no one was found worthy to open the scroll or to look into it. Then one of the elders said to me, 'Weep not; lo, the Lion of the tribe of Judah, the Root of David, has conquered, so that he can open the scroll and its seven seals (Revelation 5, 1-5)."

"I Jesus have sent my angel to you with this testimony for the churches. I am the root and offspring of David, the bright morning star (Revelation 22, 16)."

SAVIOR

The saving power of God is recounted all through sacred Scripture. However, in the person of Jesus, we see the personification or the living reality of this word.

In the Old Testament, or the Hebrew Scriptures, David calls God his "Savior."

"And David spoke to the LORD the words of this song on the day when the LORD delivered him from the hand of all his enemies, and from the hand of Saul. He said,

> 'The LORD is my rock, and my
> fortress, and my deliverer,
> my God, my rock, in whom I
>   take refuge,
> my shield and the horn of my
>   salvation,
> my stronghold and my refuge,
> my savior; thou that savest me from
>   violence.
> I call upon the LORD, who is worthy
>   to be praised,
> and I am saved from my enemies (2 Samuel 22, 1-4).''

The word "savior" in this case comes from a root word meaning to be open, wide, or free. God is the One who delivers, frees, and rescues.

Psalm 106 tells of God's greatness and the stubbornness of the people of God.

"They forgot God, their Savior,
who had done great things in
   Egypt,
wondrous works in the land of Ham,
and terrible things by the Red
   Sea (Psalm 106, 20-22)."

"But now thus says the LORD,
he who created you, O Jacob,
he who formed you, O Israel:
'Fear not, for I have redeemed
   you,
I have called you by name, you
   are mine.
When you pass through the waters
   I will be with you;
and through the rivers, they shall
   not overwhelm you;
when you walk through fire you shall
   not be burned,
and the flames shall not consume
   you.
For I am the LORD your God,
  the Holy One of Israel ,your
    Savior (Isaiah 43, 1-3a)."

"Truly thou art a God who hidest
    thyself,
O God of Israel, the Savior (Isaiah 45, 15)."

"And there is no other god besides
    me,
a righteous God and a Savior;
there is none besides me.

Turn to me and be saved,
all the ends of the earth!
For I am God, and there is no
   other (Isaiah 45, 21-22)."

> "I am the LORD your God
> from the land of Egypt;
> you know no God but me.
> and besides me there is no savior (Hosea 13, 4)."

The first reference to God as Savior comes from the lips of the Blessed Virgin Mary. Elisabeth, who is carrying in her womb John the Baptist, said to her kinswoman Mary, "Blessed is she who believed that there would be a fulfillment of what was spoken to her from the Lord." (Luke 1, 45) Mary responds,

> " 'My soul magnifies the Lord,
> and my spirit rejoices in God my
> Savior … (Luke 1, 46-47).' "

Jesus, the promised Savior, is born! "And in that region there were shepherds out in the field, keeping watch over their flock by night. And an angel of the Lord appeared to them, and the glory of the Lord shown around them, and they were filled with fear. And the angel said to them, 'Be not afraid; for behold, I bring you good news of a great joy which will come to all the people; for to you is born this day in the city of David a Savior, who is Christ the Lord (Luke 2, 8-11).' "

In the Gospel of John , there is the account of the Samaritan woman, the "woman at the well" who comes to personal faith in Jesus and then tells the people in her town all about him. Jesus stayed two days in the town. "And many more believed because of his word. They said to the woman, 'It is no longer because of your words that we believe, for we have heard for ourselves, and we know that this is indeed the Savior of the world (John 4, 41-42).' "

Peter and the apostles were brought before the rulers of the synagogue and charged with telling people about Jesus. "When they brought them in to face the Sanhedrin, the high priest demanded an explanation. 'We gave you a strong warning', he said, 'not to preach this name, and what have you done? You have filled Jerusalem with your teaching, and seem determined to fix the guilt of this man's death upon us.' In reply Peter and the apostles said, 'Obedience to God comes before obedience to men; it was the God of our ancestors who raised up Jesus, whom you executed by hanging on a tree. By his own right hand God has now raised him up to be leader and Saviour, to give repentance and forgiveness of sins through him to Israel. We are witnesses to this, we and the Holy Spirit whom God has given to those who obey him.' This so infuriated them that they wanted to put them to death (Acts 5, 28-33)."

At the synagogue at Antioch, Paul gives a brief summary of

salvation history. "So Paul stood up and with a gesture began to speak: 'You Israelites and others who fear God, listen. The God of this people Israel chose our ancestors and made the people great during their stay in the land of Egypt, and with uplifted arm he led them out of it. For about forty years he put up with them in the wilderness. After he had destroyed seven nations in the land of Canaan, he gave them their land as an inheritance for about four hundred fifty years. After that he gave them judges until the time of the prophet Samuel. Then they asked for a king; and God gave them Saul son of Kish, a man of the tribe of Benjamin, who reigned forty years. When he had removed him, he made David their king. In his testimony about him he said, 'I have found David, son of Jesse, to be a man after my heart, who will carry out all my wishes. Of this man's posterity God has brought to Israel a Savior, Jesus, as he promised; before his coming John had already proclaimed a baptism of repentance to all the people of Israel. And as John was finishing his work, he said, "What do you suppose that I am? I am not he. No, but one is coming after me; I am not worthy to untie the thong of the sandals on his feet (Acts 13, 16-25 NRSV).' "

The name "Savior" pops up in the most unexpected places. "For the husband is the head of the wife just as Christ is head of the church, the body of which he is the Savior. Husbands, love your wives just as Christ loved the church and gave himself up for her … (Ephesians 5, 23, 25 NRSV)." The Savior lives a life of constant sacrifice to protect the beloved.

"Brothers and sisters, join in imitating me, and observe those who live according to the example you have in us. For many live as enemies of the cross of Christ; I have often told you of them, and now I tell you even with tears. Their end is destruction; their god is the belly; and their glory is in their shame; their minds are set on earthly things. But our citizenship is in heaven, and it is from there that we are expecting a Savior, the Lord Jesus Christ. He will transform the body of our humiliation that it may be conformed to the body of his glory, by the power that also enables him to make all things new (Philippians 3, 17-20 NRSV)."

"First of all, then, I urge that supplications, prayers, intercessions, and thanksgivings be made for everyone, for kings and all who are in high positions, so that we may live a quite and peaceable life in all godliness and dignity. This is right and is acceptable in the sight of God our Savior, who desires everyone to be saved and to come to the knowledge of truth. For there is one God; there is also one mediator between God and humankind, Christ Jesus, himself human, who gave himself a ransom for all … (1 Timothy, 2, 1-6 NRSV)."

"... we have our hope set on the living God, who is the Savior of all people, especially of those who believe (1 Timothy 4, 10 NRSV)."

"Do not be ashamed, then, of the testimony about our Lord or of me, his prisoner, but join with me in suffering for the gospel, relying on the power of God, who saved us and called us with a holy calling, not according to our works but according to his own purpose and grace. This grace was given to us in Christ Jesus before the ages began, but it has now been revealed through the appearing of our Savior Jesus Christ, who abolished death and brought life and immortality to light through the gospel. For this gospel I was appointed a herald and an apostle and a teacher, and for this reason I suffer as I do. But I am not ashamed, for I know the one in whom I have put my trust and I am sure that he is able to guard until that day what I have entrusted to him
(2 Timothy 1, 8-12 NRSV)."

"For the grace of God has appeared, bringing salvation to all, training us to renounce impiety and worldly passions, and in the present age to live lives that are self-controlled, upright, and godly, while we wait for the blessed hope and the manifestation of the glory of our great God and Savior, Jesus Christ. He it is who gave himself for us that he might redeem us from all iniquity and purify for himself a people of his own who are zealous for good deeds. Declare these things; exhort and reprove with all authority. Let no one look down on you (Titus 2, 11-15 NRSV)."

"Remind them to be subject to rulers and authorities, to be obedient, to be ready for every good work, to speak evil of no one, to avoid quarreling, to be gentle, and to show every courtesy to everyone. For we ourselves were once foolish, disobedient, led astray, slaves to various passions and pleasures, passing our days in malice and envy, despicable, hating one another. But when the goodness and loving kindness of God our Savior appeared, he saved us, not because of any works of righteousness that we had done, but according to his mercy, through the water of rebirth and renewal by the Holy Spirit. This Spirit he poured out on us richly through Jesus Christ our Savior, so that, having been justified by his grace, we might become heirs according to the hope of eternal life (Titus 3, 1-7 NRSV)."

"... you must make every effort to support your faith with goodness, and goodness with knowledge, and knowledge with self-control, and self-control with endurance, and endurance with godliness, and godliness with mutual affection, and mutual affection with love. For if these things are yours and are increasing among you, they keep you from being ineffective and unfruitful in the knowledge of our Lord Jesus Christ. For anyone who lacks these things is nearsighted and blind, and is forgetful of the cleansing of past sins. Therefore, brothers and sisters, be all the more eager to confirm your call and election, for if you do this, you will never stumble. For in this way, entry into the eternal kingdom of our Lord and Savior Jesus Christ will be richly provided for you (2 Peter 1, 5-11 NRSV)."

"... people are slaves to whatever masters them. For if, after they have escaped the defilements of the world through the knowledge of our Lord and Savior Jesus Christ, they are again entangled in them and overpowered, the last state has become worse for them than the first. For it would have been better for them never to have known the way of righteousness than, after knowing it, to turn back from the holy commandment that was passed on to them (2 Peter 2, 19b-21 NRSV)."

"... grow in the grace and knowledge of our Lord and Savior Jesus Christ. To him be the glory both now and to the day of eternity (2 Peter 3, 18 NRSV)."

"And we have seen and do testify that the Father has sent his Son as the Savior of the world. God abides in those who confess that Jesus is the Son of God, and they abide in God. So we have known and believe the love that God has for us (1 John 4, 14-16 NRSV)."

"Now to him who is able to keep you from falling and to present you without blemish before the presence of his glory with rejoicing, to the only God, our Savior through Jesus Christ our LORD, be glory, majesty, dominion, and authority, before all time and now and for ever." (Jude 24-25)

SERVANT

In the Hebrew Scriptures, or the Old Testament, it would be unthinkable to refer to God as a servant. The closest to this would be in Isaiah 42, the first "Servant Song" and in Isaiah 53, the "suffering servant" chapter. Many see this servant as a reference to the coming Messiah.

> "Behold my servant, whom I
>   uphold,
> my chosen, in whom my soul
>   delights;
> I have put my Spirit upon him,
> he will bring forth justice to the
>   nations.
> He will not cry or lift up his voice,
>   or make it heard in the street;
> a bruised reed he will not break,

and a dimly burning wick he will
   not quench;
he will faithfully bring forth
   justice (Isaiah 42, 1-3)."

"Who has believed what we
have heard?
   And to whom has the arm of the
     LORD been revealed?
For he grew up before him like a
   young plant,
and like a root out of dry ground;
he had no form or comeliness that
   we should look at him,
and no beauty that we should desire him.
He was despised and rejected by
   men;
a man of sorrows and acquainted
   with grief;
and as one from whom men hide
   their faces
he was despised, and we esteemed
   him not.

Surely he has borne our griefs
   and carried our sorrows;
yet we esteemed him stricken,
smitten by God, and afflicted.
But he was wounded for our
   transgressions,
he was bruised for our iniquities;
upon him was the chastisement that
   made us whole,
and with his stripes we are healed.
All we like sheep have gone astray;
we have turned every one to his
   own way;
and the LORD has laid on him
the iniquity of us all.

He was oppressed, and he was afflicted,
   yet he opened not his mouth;
like a lamb that is led to the
   slaughter,
and like a sheep that before its
   shearers is dumb,

so he opened not his mouth.

By oppression and judgment he was
 taken away;
and as for his generation, who
 considered
that he was cut off out of the land
 of the living,
stricken for the transgression of
 my people?
And they made his grave with the
 wicked
and with a rich man in his death,
although he had done no violence,
 and there was no deceit in his
  mouth.

Yet it was the will of the LORD to
 bruise him;
he has put him to grief;
when he makes himself an offering
 for sin,
he shall see his offspring, he shall
 prolong his days;
the will of the LORD shall prosper
 in his hand;
he shall see the fruit of the travail
 of his soul and be satisfied;
by his knowledge shall the righteous one,
 my servant,
make many to be accounted righteous;
and he shall bear their iniquities.
Therefore I will divide a portion
 with the great,
and he shall divide the spoil with
 the strong;
because he poured out his soul to
 death,
and was numbered with the
 transgressors;
yet he bore the sin of many,
 and made intercession for the
  transgressors (Isaiah 53, 1-12)."

In the New Testament, the first reference to Jesus as a servant is in Matthew's Gospel. This is a reference to the Isaiah 53 passage.

"And many followed him, and he healed them all, and ordered them not to make him known. This was to fulfill what was spoken by the prophet Isaiah:

> 'Behold, my servant whom I have
>   chosen,
> my beloved with whom my soul
>   is well pleased.
> I will put my spirit upon him,
> and he shall proclaim justice to the
>   Gentiles.
> He will not wrangle or cry aloud,
> nor will any one hear his voice
>   in the streets;
> he will not break a bruised reed
> or quench a smoldering wick,
> till he brings justice to victory;
> and in his name will the
>   Gentiles hope (Matthew 12, 15b-21).' "

"Whoever would be great among you must be your servant, and whoever would be first among you must be your slave; even as the Son of man came not to be served but to serve, and to give his life as a ransom for many (Matthew 20, 26b-28)."

"The greatest among you will be your servant. All who exalt themselves will be humbled, and all who humble themselves will be exalted (Matthew 23, 11-12 NRSV)."

Jesus said to his disciples, " 'If any one would be first, he must be last of all and servant of all.' And he took a child, and put him in the midst of them; and taking him in his arms, he said to them, 'Whoever receives one such child in my name receives not me but him who sent me (Mark 9, 35b-37).' "

When James and John were asking for special honor, Jesus said to them, " '... whoever would be great among you must be your servant, and whoever would be first among you must be slave of all. For the Son of man also came not to be served but to serve, and to give his life as a ransom for many (Mark 10, 44).' "

Jesus, in love and humility, washes the feet of his disciples. This is usually the task, not merely of a servant, but of the lowliest slave.

"Jesus, knowing that the Father had given all things into his hands, and that he had come from God and was going to God, rose from supper, laid aside his garments, and girded himself with a towel. Then he poured water into a basin, and began to wash the disciples' feet, and to wipe them with the towel with which he was girded. He came to Simon Peter; and Peter said to him, 'Lord, do you wash my feet?' Jesus answered him, 'What I am doing you do not know now, but afterward you will understand.' Peter said to him, 'You shall never wash my feet.' Jesus answered him, 'If I do not wash you, you have no part in me.' Simon Peter said to him, 'Lord, not my feet only but also my hands and my head!' Jesus said to him, 'He who has bathed does not need to wash, except for his feet, but he is clean all over; and you are clean, but not every one of you.' For he knew who was to betray him; that was why he said, 'You are not all clean.'

When he had washed their feet, and taken his garments, and resumed his place, he said to them, 'Do you know what I have done to you?' You call me Teacher and Lord, and you are right, for so I am. If I then, your Lord and Teacher, have washed your feet, you also ought to wash one another's feet. For I have given you an example, that you also should do as I have done to you.' Truly, truly, I say to you, a servant is not greater than his master; not is he who is sent greater than he who sent him. If you know these things, blessed are you if you do them (John 13, 3-17).' "

After the lame man was healed at the Beautiful Gate of the Temple, Peter addressed the people.

"… You Israelites, why do you wonder at this, or why do you stare at us, as though by our own power or piety we had made him walk? The God of Abraham, the God of Isaac, and the God of Jacob, the God of our ancestors has glorified his servant, Jesus, whom you handed over and rejected in the presence of Pilate, though he had decided to release him. But you rejected the Holy and Righteous One and asked to have a murderer given to you, and you killed the Author of life, whom God raised from the dead, To this we are witnesses (Acts 3, 12-15 NRSV)."

"Let the same mind be in you that was in Christ Jesus, who, though he was in the form of God, did not regard equality with God as something to be exploited, but emptied himself, taking the form of a slave, being born in human likeness. And being found in human form, he humbled himself and became obedient to the point of death – even death on a cross. Therefore God also highly exalted him and gave him the name that is above every name, so that at the name of Jesus every knee should bend, in heaven and on earth and under the earth, and every tongue should confess that Jesus Christ is Lord, to the glory of God the Father (Philippians 2, 5-11 NRSV)."

SHEPHERD

The image of Jesus as shepherd, especially of Jesus as the Good Shepherd, is one of great tenderness and great strength. In the arms of Jesus, the little lamb has only to rest secure.

Ann, my Ukrainian godmother, a registered nurse, once told me of her time in the hospital as a patient herself. She could not sleep. One night she began to see herself as a lamb being held close to the heart of Jesus. It was so real to her that she could almost hear his heart beating. She fell peacefully asleep. She recovered and resumed her vocation. The image of the little lamb resting safely in the arms of Jesus, the Good Shepherd, has helped many people.

"The LORD is my shepherd,
   I shall not want;
he makes me lie down in green pastures.
He leads me beside still waters;
   he restores my soul.
He leads me in paths of righteousness
   for his name's sake.

Even though I walk through the
valley of the shadow of death,
I fear no evil;
for thou art with me;
thy rod and thy staff,
   they comfort me.

Thou preparest a table before me
in the presence of my enemies;
thou anointest my head with oil,
   my cup overflows.
Surely goodness and mercy shall
   follow me
all the days of my life;
and I shall dwell in the house of the
   LORD
for ever (Psalm 23)."

"You guided your people like a flock
   by the hand of Moses and Aaron (Psalm 77, 20)."

"Give ear, O Shepherd of Israel,
   thou who leadest Joseph like a
     flock!

> Thou who art enthroned upon the
> cherubim, shine forth
> before Ephraim and Benjamin
> and Manasseh!
> Stir up thy might,
> and come to save us (Psalm 80, 1-2)!"

"Behold, the LORD God comes with
    might,
and his arm rules for him;
behold, his reward is with him,
and his recompense before him.
He will feed his flock like a
    shepherd,
he will gather the lambs in his
    arms,
he will carry them in his bosom,
and gently lead those that are with
    young (Isaiah 40, 10-11)."

The two verses above present a balanced view of the character of God. There is both the sense of power and authority and the sense of gentleness and tenderness.

"Hear the word of the LORD, O nations, and declare it in the coast lands far away; say, 'He who scattered Israel will gather him, and will keep him as a shepherd a flock. For the LORD has ransomed Jacob, and has redeemed him from hands too strong for him. They shall come and sing aloud on the height of Zion, and they shall be radiant over the goodness of the LORD, over the grain, the wine, and the oil, and over the young of the flock and the herd; their life shall become like a watered garden, and they shall never languish again. Then shall the young women rejoice in the dance, and the young men and the old shall be merry. I will turn their mourning into joy, I will comfort them and give them gladness for sorrow (Jeremiah 31, 10-13 NRSV)."

In Ezekiel 34, the Lord God speaks against and condemns the "shepherds" (rulers) of Israel who have misused their authority and not cared for the "flock."

"The word of the LORD came to me: 'Son of man, prophesy against the shepherds of Israel, prophesy, and say to them, even to the shepherds, 'Thus says the LORD God, Ho, shepherds of Israel who have been feeding yourselves! Should not shepherds feed the sheep? You eat the fat, you clothe yourselves with the wool, you slaughter the fatlings; but you do not feed the sheep. The weak you have not strengthened, the sick you have not healed, the cripple you have not bound up, the strayed you have not brought back, the lost you have not sought, and with force and harshness you have ruled them. So they were scattered, because there was no shepherd; and they became food for all the wild beasts. My sheep were scattered, they wandered over all the mountains and on every high hill; my sheep were scattered over all the face of the earth, with none to search or to seek for them.

'Therefore, you shepherds, hear the word of the LORD: As I live, says the LORD GOD, because my sheep have become a prey, and my sheep have become food for all the wild beasts, since there was no shepherd; and because my shepherds have not searched for my sheep, but the shepherds have fed themselves, and have not fed my sheep; therefore, you shepherds, hear the word of the LORD: 'Thus says the LORD GOD, Behold, I am against the shepherds; and I will require my sheep at their hand, and put a stop to their feeding the sheep; no longer shall the shepherds feed themselves. I will rescue the sheep from their mouths, that they may not be food for them.

'For thus says the LORD God: Behold, I myself will search for my sheep, and will seek them out. As a shepherd seeks out his flock when some of his sheep have been scattered abroad, so will I seek out my sheep; and I will rescue them from all places where they have been scattered on a day of clouds and thick darkness. And I will bring them out from the peoples, and gather them from the countries, and will bring them into their own land; and I will feed them on the mountains of Israel, by the fountains, and in all the inhabited places of the country. I will feed them with good pasture, and upon the mountain heights of Israel shall be their pasture; there they shall lie down in good grazing land, and on fat pasture they shall feed on the mountains of Israel. I myself will be the shepherd of my sheep, and I will make them lie down, says the LORD GOD. I will seek the lost, and I will bring back the strayed, and I will bind up the crippled, and I will strengthen the weak, and the fat and the strong I will watch over; I will feed them in justice.

'I will save my flock, they shall no longer be a prey; and I will judge between sheep and sheep. And I will set up over them one shepherd, my servant David, and he shall feed them and be their shepherd. And I, the LORD, will be their God, and my servant David shall be prince among them; I, the LORD, have spoken (Ezekiel 34, 1-16, 22-24).' "

> "... the people wander like
>   sheep;
> they suffer for lack of a
>   shepherd. My anger is hot against the
>   shepherds,

> and I will punish the leaders;
> for the LORD of hosts cares for his
>   flock … (Zechariah 10, 2c-3b NRSV)."

We turn now to the New Testament to consider some of the references about Jesus as the Good Shepherd.

"When the Son of man comes in his glory, and all the angels with him, then he will sit on his glorious throne. Before him will be gathered all the nations, and he will separate them one from another as a shepherd separates the sheep from the goats, and he will place the sheep at his right hand, but the goats at the left. Then the King will say to those at his right hand, 'Come, O blessed of my Father, inherit the kingdom prepared for you from the foundation of the world; for I was hungry and you gave me food, I was thirsty and you gave me drink, I was a stranger and you welcomed me, I was naked and you clothed me, I was sick and you visited me, I was in prison and you came to me.' Then the righteous will answer him, 'Lord, when did we see thee hungry and feed thee, or thirsty and give thee a drink? And when did we see thee a stranger and welcome thee, or naked and clothe thee? And when did we see thee sick or in prison and visit them? And the King will answer them, 'Truly, I say to you, as you did it to one of the least of these my brethren, you did it to me (Matthew 25, 31-40).' "

" 'Very truly, I tell you, anyone who does not enter the sheepfold by the gate but climbs in by another way is a thief and a bandit. The one who enters by the gate is the shepherd of the sheep. The gatekeeper opens the gate for him, and the sheep hear his voice. He calls his own sheep by name and leads them out. When he as brought out all his own, he goes ahead of them, and the sheep follow him because they know his voice, They will not follow a stranger, but they will run from him because they do not know the voice of strangers.' Jesus used this figure of speech with them, but they did not understand what he was saying to them. So again Jesus said to them, 'Very truly, I tell you, I am the gate for the sheep. All who came before me are thieves and bandits; but the sheep did not listen to them. I am the gate, Whoever enters by me will be saved, and will come in and go out and find pasture. The thief comes only to steal and kill and destroy. I have come that they may have life, and have it abundantly. I am the good shepherd. The good shepherd lays down his life for the sheep. The hired hand, who is not the shepherd and does not own the sheep, sees the wolf coming and leaves the sheep and runs away – and the wolf snatches them and scatters them. The hired hand runs away because a hired hand does not care for the sheep. I am the good shepherd. I know my own and my own know me, just as the Father knows me and I know the Father. And I lay down my life for the sheep. I have other sheep that do not belong to this fold. I must bring them also, and they will listen to my voice. So there will be one flock, one shepherd (John 10. 1-16 (NRSV).'"

"Now may the God of peace who brought again from the dead our LORD Jesus, the great shepherd of the sheep, by the blood of the eternal covenant, equip you with everything good that you may do his will, working in you that which is pleasing in his sight, through Jesus Christ; to whom be glory for ever and ever. Amen. (Hebrews 13, 20-21)."

"... if when you do right and suffer for it you take it patiently, you have God's approval. For to this you have been called, because Christ also suffered for you, leaving you an example, that you should follow in his steps. He committed no sin, no guile was found on his lips. When he was reviled, he did not revile in return; when he suffered, he did not threaten; but he trusted to him who judges justly. He himself bore our sins in his body on the tree, that we might die to sin and live to righteousness. By his wounds you have been healed. For you were straying like sheep, but have now returned to the Shepherd and Guardian of your souls (1 Peter 2, 20b-25)."

"So I exhort the elders among you, as a fellow elder and a witness of the sufferings of Christ as well as a partaker in the glory that is to be revealed. Tend the flock of God that is your charge, not by constraint but willingly, not for shameful gain but eagerly, not as domineering over those in your charge but being examples to the flock. And when the chief Shepherd is manifest you will obtain the unfading crown of glory. Likewise you that are younger be subject to the elders. Clothe yourselves, all of you, with humility toward one another, for God opposes the proud, but gives grace to the humble (1 Peter 5, 1-5)."

SHIELD

In a number of places in the Old Testament, God is referred to as a "shield."

"... the word of the LORD came to Abram in a vision,

'Fear not, Abram, I am your shield;
your reward shall be very great (Genesis 15, 1).'"

"Happy are you, O Israel! Who is
like you,
a people saved by the LORD,
the shield of your help,
and the sword of your triumph (Deuteronomy 33, 29a)!"

"And David spoke to the LORD the words of this song on the day when the LORD delivered him from the hand of all his enemies, and from the hand of Saul. He said,

'The LORD is my rock,
  and my fortress, and
    my deliverer,
  my God, my rock, in whom I
    take refuge,
  my shield and the horn of my
    salvation,
  my stronghold and my refuge,
  my savior; thou savest me from
    violence (2 Samuel 22, 1-3).' "

"O LORD, how many are my foes!
  Many are rising against me;
    many are saying to me,
  'There is no help for you in God.'
    But you, O LORD, are a shield around me,
      my glory, and the one who lifts up my head
        (Psalm 3, 1-3 NRSV)."

"The LORD is my strength and my
    shield;
  in him my heart trusts;
    so I am helped, and my heart exults,
      and with my song I give thanks to
        him (Psalm 28, 7)."

"Our soul waits for the LORD;
  he is our help and our shield (Psalm 33, 20)."

"For the LORD God is a sun and
    shield;
  he bestows favor and honor.
  No good thing does the LORD
    withhold
  from those who walk uprightly (Psalm 84, 11)."

"O Israel, trust in the LORD!
    He is their help and their shield.
  O house of Aaron, put your trust in
    the LORD!
  He is their help and their shield.
  You who fear the LORD, trust in

the LORD!
He is their help and their shield (Psalm 115, 9-11)."

"Thou art my hiding place and my
   shield;
I hope in thy word (Psalm 119, 114)."

"Blessed be the LORD, my
   rock,
who trains my hands for war,
   and my fingers for battle;
my rock and my fortress,
my stronghold and my deliverer,
   my shield and he in whom I take
      refuge ... (Psalm 144, 1-2)."

"Every word of God proves true;
   he is a shield to those who take
      refuge in him (Proverbs 30, 5)."

SON

Jesus is referred to as both Son of God (referring to his divinity) and Son of Man (referring to his humanity). He is Son of God and son of Mary. He is the only One who can understand us perfectly, because he was and is both fully human and fully divine.

The coming of the messianic king was prophesied in the book of Isaiah.

"For to us a child is born,
   to us a son is given;
and the government will be upon
   his shoulder,
and his name shall be called
   'Wonderful Counselor, Mighty God,
Everlasting Father, Prince of
   Peace (Isaiah 9, 6).'"

Do you remember the story of King Nebuchadnezzar throwing Daniel's three friends Shadrach, Meschach, and Abednego into the fiery furnace because they refused bow down and worship the golden image? The flames were so hot that the men who threw the three friends in the furnace were themselves killed. But of the three? "Then King Nebuchadnezzar was astonished and rose up in haste. He said to his counselors, 'Did we not cast three men bound into the fire?' They answered, 'True, O King.' He answered, 'But I see four men loose, walking in the midst of the fire, and they are not hurt; and the appearance of the fourth is like a son of the gods (Daniel 3, 24-25).' "

Daniel later has a vision of the passing of earthly kingdoms in order to prepare for the coming of God's kingdom.

> "As I looked,
>   thrones were placed
> and one that was ancient of days
>   took his seat;
> his raiment was white as snow,
> and the hair of his head like pure
>   wool;
> his throne was fiery flames,
> its wheels were burning fire.
> A stream of fire issued
> and came forth from before him;
> a thousand thousands served him;
> the court sat in judgment,
>   and the books were opened.
> I looked then because of the sound of the great words
> which the horn was speaking. And as I looked, the beast
> was slain, and its body destroyed and given over to be
> burned with fire. As for the rest of the beasts, their
> dominion was taken away, but their lives were prolonged
>   for a season and a time.
> I saw in the night visions,
> and behold, with the clouds of
>   heaven
> there came one like a son of man,
> and he came to the Ancient of Days
>   and was presented before him.
> And to him was given dominion
> and glory and kingdom,
> that all peoples, nations, and
>   languages
> should serve him;
> his dominion is an everlasting dominion,
> which shall not pass away,
> and his kingdom one
>   that shall not be destroyed.
> 'As for me, Daniel, my spirit within me was
> anxious and the visions of my head alarmed me.
> I approached

one of those who stood there and asked him the truth concerning all this. So he told me, and made known to me the interpretation of the things.
'These four beasts are four great kings who shall arise out of the earth. But the saints of the Most High shall receive the kingdom, and possess the kingdom for ever, for ever and ever (Daniel 7, 9-18).'"

My favorite Gospel, since childhood, the Gospel of Saint John, plunges us into the reality of the divinity of Christ.

"No one has ever seen God. It is God the only Son, who is close to the Father's heart, who has made him known (John 1, 18 NRSV)."

The Gospel of Matthew gives the human genealogy of Jesus, referring to him as the "son of David (Matthew 1, 1)."

"Now the birth of Jesus Christ took place in this way. When his mother Mary had been betrothed to Joseph, before they came together she was found to be with child of the Holy Spirit; and her husband Joseph, being a just man and unwilling to put her to shame, resolved to divorce her quietly. But as he considered this, behold, an angel of the Lord appeared to him in a dream, saying, 'Joseph, son of David, do not fear to take Mary your wife, for that which is conceived in her is of the Holy Spirit; she will bear a son, and you shall call his name Jesus, for he will save his people from their sins.' All this took place to fulfill what the Lord had spoken by the prophet:

'Behold, a virgin shall conceive and
  bear a son,
and his name shall be called
  Emmanuel'
    (which means, God with us) (Matthew 1, 18-25).'"

Jesus, as an infant, was taken by Mary and Joseph to Egypt to escape from Herod, the cruel king, who was planning to murder all the male infants in the region of Bethlehem. The king was hoping, by this means, to make sure that Jesus was among the slain. God always has the last word, however.

"... an angel of the Lord appeared to Joseph in a dream and said, 'Rise, take the child and his mother, and flee to Egypt, and remain there till I tell you; for Herod is about to search for the child to destroy him.' And he rose and took the child and his mother by night, and departed to Egypt, and remained there until the death of Herod. This was to fulfill what the Lord had spoken by the prophet, 'Out of Egypt have I called my son (Matthew 2, 13-15).' "

The term "Son" is of particular significance during the baptism of Jesus. Jesus, although completely sinless, submitted to baptism in order to identify himself with his those who were responding to God through the ministry of John the Baptist.

"Then Jesus came from Galilee to the Jordan to John, to be baptized by him. John would have prevented him, saying, 'I need to be baptized by you, and do you come to me?' But Jesus answered him, 'Let it be so for now; for thus it is fitting for us to fulfill all righteousness.' Then he consented. And when Jesus was baptized, he went up immediately from the water, and behold the heavens were opened and he saw the Spirit of God descending like a dove, and alighting on him; and lo, a voice from heaven, saying, 'This is my beloved Son, with whom I am well pleased (Matthew 3, 13-17).' "

The baptism of Jesus is also recounted in the Gospels of Mark (Mark 1, 9-11) and Luke (Luke 3, 21-22).

The detail of Jesus at prayer is added in Luke's Gospel.

"Now when all the people were baptized, and when Jesus also had been baptized and was praying, the heaven was opened, and the Holy Spirit descended upon him in bodily form, as a dove, and a voice came from heaven, 'Thou art my beloved Son; with thee I am well pleased (Luke 21, 21-22).' "

John the Baptist referred to Jesus as both Lamb of God and Son of God. "And John testified, 'I saw the Spirit descending from heaven like a dove, and remain on him [Jesus]. I myself did not know him, but the one who sent me to baptize with water said to me, 'He on whom you see the Spirit descend and remain is the one who baptizes with the Holy Spirit.' And I myself have seen and have testified that this is the Son of God (John 1, 32-34 NRSV).' "

As soon as Jesus was baptized and his identity was proclaimed, temptation began.

"Then Jesus was led up by the Spirit into the wilderness to be tempted by the devil. He fasted forty days and forty nights, and afterwards he was famished. The tempter came to him and said to him. 'If you are the Son of God, command these stones to become loaves of bread.' But he answered, 'It is written, 'One does not live by bread alone, but by every word that comes from the mouth of God.' Then the devil took him to the holy city and placed him on the pinnacle of the temple, saying to him, 'If you are the Son of God, throw yourself down; for it is written, 'He will command his angels concerning you,' and 'On their hands they will bear you up, so that you will not dash your foot against a stone.' Jesus said to him, 'Again it is written, 'Do not put the Lord your God to the test. Again, the devil took him to a very high mountain and showed him all the kingdoms of the world and their splendor; and he said to him, 'All these things I will give you, if you will fall down and worship me.' Jesus said, 'Away with you, Satan! for it is written, 'Worship the Lord your God and serve only him.' Then the devil left him, and suddenly angels came and waited on him (Matthew 4, 1-11 NRSV)."

The Gospel of Mark has very strong language about Jesus going into the wilderness. Immediately after his baptism, "… the Spirit immediately drove him out into the wilderness. He was in the wilderness forty days, tempted by Satan; and he was with the wild beasts; and the angels waited on him (Mark 1, 12-14 NRSV)."

This is how Satan attacks. When God says something, in this case, "This is my beloved Son," Satan comes to plant questions and doubts ("If you are…").

The way Jesus dealt with Satan is the way we can deal with this evil entity. Proclaim, as Jesus, did, what GOD said.

Satan is clever; he quotes Scripture. But he quotes it with intent to distort. Jesus puts Scripture in total context of who God is and what God is saying to us.

Jesus wants to make sure that those who would follow him are fully aware that it will not be an easy life.

"Now when Jesus saw great crowds around him, he gave orders to go over to the other side. And a scribe came up and said to him, 'Teacher, I will follow you wherever you go.' And Jesus said to him, 'Foxes have holes, and birds of the air have nests; but the Son of man has nowhere to lay his head (Matthew 8, 18-20).' " This passage is also recounted in Luke 9, 57-60.

"And when he came to the other side, to the country of the Gadarenes, two demoniacs met him, coming out of the tombs, so fierce that no one could pass that way. And behold, they cried out, 'What have you to do with us, O Son of God? Have you come here to torment us before the time (Matthew 8, 28-29)?' "

The account of the Gadarene demoniacs is also found in Mark 5,

1-20 and in Luke 8, 26-39.

Evil spirits knew who Jesus really was -- that he was divine, that he was the Son of God as well as the Son of Man. They were frightened because they knew he had ultimate power and authority over them.

"And after getting into a boat he crossed the sea and came to his own town. And just then some people were carrying a paralyzed man lying on a bed. When Jesus saw their faith, he said to the paralytic, 'Take heart, son; your sins are forgiven.' Then some of the scribes said to themselves, 'This man is blaspheming.' But Jesus, perceiving their thoughts, said, 'Why do you think evil in your hearts? For which is easier, to say, 'Your sins are forgiven,' or to say, 'Stand up and walk'? But that you may know that the Son of Man has authority on earth to forgive sins – he then said to the paralytic – 'Stand up, take your bed and go to your home.' And he stood up and went to his home. When the crowds saw it, they were filled with awe, and they glorified God, who had given such authority to human beings (Matthew 9-1-8 NRSV)."

The account of the healing of the paralytic is also found in Mark 2, 1-12 and in Luke 5, 17-26. Jesus, in all three accounts, chooses to refer to himself as Son of man.

Jesus was sometimes called "Son of David, " a term understood by the Jews as a messianic title.

"And as Jesus passed on from there, two blind men followed him, crying aloud, 'Have mercy on us, Son of David.' And when he entered the house, the blind men came to him; and Jesus said to them, 'Do you believe that I am able to do this?' They said to him, 'Yes, Lord.' Then he touched their eyes, saying 'According to your faith be it done to you,' And their eyes were opened. And Jesus sternly charged them, 'See that no one know it.' But they went away and spread his fame through all that district (Matthew 9, 27-31)."

In the accounts in Mark 10, 46-52 and in Luke 18, 35-43, Jesus is also addressed by the blind beggars as Son of David.

"At that time Jesus said, 'I thank you, Father, Lord of heaven and earth, because you have hidden these things from the wise and intelligent and have revealed them to infants; yes, Father, for such was your gracious will. All things have been handed over to me by my Father; and no one knows the Son except the Father, and no one knows the Father except the Son and anyone to whom the Son chooses to reveal him. 'Come to me, all you that are weary and are carrying heavy burdens, and I will give you rest. Take my yoke upon you, and learn from me; for I am gentle and humble in heart, and you will find rest for your souls. For my yoke is easy, and my burden is light (Matthew 11, 25-30 NRSV).' "

"At that time Jesus went through the grainfields on the sabbath; his disciples were hungry, and they began to pluck heads of grain and to eat. But when the Pharisees saw it, they said to him, 'Look, your disciples are doing what is not lawful to do on the sabbath. He said to them, 'Have you not read what David did, when he was hungry, and those who were with him: how he entered the house of God and ate the bread of the Presence, which it was not lawful for him to eat nor for those who were with him, but only for the priests? Or have you not read in the law how on the sabbath the priests in the temple profane the sabbath, and are guiltless. For the Son of man is lord of the sabbath (Matthew 12, 1-8)."

The plucking of the grains of wheat on the sabbath is also told in Mark 2, 23-28 and in Luke 1, 1-5. Mark adds the words of Jesus that "… the sabbath was made for humankind, and not humankind for the sabbath … (Mark 2, 27)."

Jesus said, " 'Anyone who is not with me is against me, and anyone who does not gather in with me throws away. And so I tell you, every human sin and blasphemy will be forgiven, but blasphemy against the Spirit will not be forgiven. And anyone who speaks against the Son of man will be forgiven; but no one who speaks against the Holy Spirit will be forgiven either in this world or in the next (Matthew 12, 30-32).' "

This is a frightening passage! People start wondering if they have committed the "unpardonable" sin. Some believe that if you are even concerned that you may have, this is a sure sign that you haven't! More likely, it means that to ascribe to Satan the works of God is the unforgivable sin. Flagrant rebellion against God is at the heart of this sin.

"Then some of the scribes and Pharisees said to him, 'Teacher, we wish to see a sign from you.' But he answered, 'An evil and adulterous generation asks for a sign, but no sign will be given to it except the sign of the prophet Jonah. For just as Jonah was three days and three nights in the belly of the sea monster, so for three days and three nights the Son of Man will be in the heart of the earth. The people of Ninevah will rise up at the judgment with this generation and condemn it, because they repented at the proclamation of Jonah, and see, something greater than Jonah is here! The queen of the South will rise up at the judgment with this generation and condemn it, because she came from the ends of the earth to listen to the wisdom of Solomon, and see, something greater than Solomon is here (Matthew 12, 38-42 NRSV).' " This passage is also recounted in Luke 11, 29-32 in which Jesus also refers to himself as Son of man.

Jesus taught the people by telling stories called parables. One of the parables was about the weeds among the wheat. He told his disciples what this meant.

"… 'The one who sows the good seed is the Son of Man; and the field is the world, and the good seed are the children of the kingdom; the weeds are the children of the evil one, and the enemy who sowed them is the devil; the harvest is the end of the age, and the reapers are angels. Just as the weeds are collected and burned up with fire, so will it be at the end of the age. The Son of Man will send his angels, and they will collect out of his kingdom all causes of sin and all evildoers, and they will throw them into the furnace of fire, where there will be weeping and gnashing of teeth. Then the righteous will shine like the sun in the kingdom of their Father. Let anyone who has ears listen (Matthew 13, 27-43 NRSV)!' "

People just couldn't figure Jesus out! The Gospel tells us that "… when Jesus had finished these parables, he went away from there, and coming to his own country he taught them in the synagogue, so that they were astonished, and said, 'Where did this man get this wisdom, and these mighty works? Is this not the carpenter's son? Is not his mother called Mary? And are not his brothers James and Joseph and Simon and Judas? And are not all his sisters with us? Where then did this man get all this? And they took offense at him. But Jesus said to them, 'A prophet is not without honor except in his own country and in his own house.' And he did not do many mighty works there, because of their unbelief (Matthew 13, 53-58)."

The New Jerusalem Bible uses even stronger language in this passage. The prophet is not simply "without honor," but is referred to as actually being "despised."

I find the above passage very challenging. How often, when we do not understand others, do we "take offense" and write them off? Maybe there is something God wants to show us through another person. Even if we don't like them or understand them, at least we can ask, "God, what is that you are trying to show me through that person's life?"

Some time ago, an English Jesuit priest was traveling in America and was asked to preside and to preach one Sunday morning at Mass on a university campus. The Gospel for that day was the one about the parable of the tenants in the vineyard. The priest asked, "Killed any prophets recently?" He explained that nowadays we "kill" prophets by "rubbishing" them, in other words, by destroying their reputations.

Jesus needed his times of solitude. He instructed his disciples to go ahead of him to the other side of the lake. "And after he had dismissed the crowds, he went up on the mountain by himself to pray. When evening came, he was there alone, but the boat by this time was many furlongs distant from the land, beaten by the waves; for the wind was against them. And in the fourth watch of the night he came to them, walking on the sea. But when the disciples saw him walking on the sea, they were terrified, saying, 'It is a ghost!' And they cried out for fear. But immediately he spoke to them, saying, 'Take heart, it is I; Have no fear.'

And Peter answered him, 'Lord, if is you, bid me come to you on the water.' He said, 'Come.' So Peter got out of the boat and walked on the water and came to Jesus; but when he saw the wind, he was afraid, and beginning to sink he cried out, 'Lord, save me.' Jesus immediately reached out his hand and caught him, saying to him, 'O man of little faith, why did you doubt?' And when they got into the boat, the wind ceased. And those in the boat worshiped him, saying, 'Truly you are the Son of God (Matthew 14, 28-33).' "

Peter had even more reason to worship Jesus! He was the only one to venture out of the safety of the boat and to go to Jesus. How is Jesus calling you to "walk on water" and go to him in trust? He is reaching out his hand to you. You are safe when you take hold of the hand of Jesus.

People of other backgrounds came to Jesus because they knew he could help them. He was in the seaside district of Tyre and Sidon. "And behold, a Canaanite woman from that region came out and cried, 'Have mercy on me, O Lord, Son of David; my daughter is severely possessed by a demon.' And he did not answer her a word. And his disciples came and begged him, saying, 'Send her away, for she is crying after us.' He answered, 'I was sent only to the lost sheep of the house of Israel.' But she came and knelt before him, saying, 'Lord, help me.' And he answered, 'It is not fair to take the children's bread and throw it to the dogs.' She said, 'Yes, Lord, yet even the dogs eat the crumbs that fall from their masters' table.' Then Jesus answered her, 'O woman, great is your faith! Be it done for you as you desire.' And her daughter was healed instantly (Matthew 15, 22-28)."

This story of the Canaanite woman is powerful! Although the Jews would have considered her as a "dog," an outsider, a nobody, she dared to address Jesus as "Son of David," in other words, as the Messiah of the Jews. She had great humility and great persistence. She knew he could heal her daughter and she intended to stick around until he did so! Jesus responded to her, not because she was a Jew, one of the "house of Israel," but because she confronted him directly with her humility and with her need. Jesus responded to her, praising her for her faith and trust and by healing her child.

The question was asked over and over, "Who in the world was this Jesus? He seemed like a regular person, the carpenter of Nazareth, yet he went about doing the most extraordinary things. He healed sick people, whether they were suffering in mind or body or both. He even forgave sins! Who was he?

As he began to call his disciples, there were different opinions about his identity. "Philip found Nathanael and said to him, 'We have found him about whom Moses in the law and also the prophets wrote, Jesus son of Joseph from Nazareth. Nathanael said to him, 'Can anything good come out of Nazareth?' Philip said to him, Come and see.' When Jesus saw Nathanael coming toward him, he said, 'Here is truly an Israelite in whom there is no deceit!' Nathanael asked him, 'Where did you get to know me?' Jesus answered, "I saw you under the fig tree before Philip called you.' Nathanael replied, 'Rabbi, you are the King of Israel!' Jesus answered, 'Do you believe because I told you that I saw you under the fig tree? You will see greater things than these.' And he said to him, 'Very truly I tell you, you will see heaven opened and the angels of God ascending and descending upon the Son of Man (John 1, 45-51 NRSV).' "

Jesus had a most remarkable conversation with a Jewish leader, Nicodemus. Nicodemus believed Jesus was a rabbi, a teacher, yet one who performed great signs. Jesus led Nicodemus into a deeper understanding of who he, Jesus, really was.

"No one has ascended into heaven except the one who descended from heaven, the Son of Man. And just as Moses lifted up the serpent in the wilderness, so must the Son of Man be lifted up, that whoever believes in him may have eternal life. For God so loved the world that he gave his only Son, so that everyone who believes in him may have eternal life. Indeed, God did not send the Son into the world to condemn the world, but in order that the world might be saved through him (John 3, 13-17 NRSV)."

Jesus made it clear that he lived and ministered according to the plan of God, his Father. " 'Very truly, I tell you, the Son can do nothing on his own, but only what he sees the Father doing; for whatever the Father does, the Son does likewise. The Father loves the Son and shows him all that he himself is doing; and he will show him greater works than these, so that you will be astonished. Indeed, just as the Father raises the dead and gives them life, so also the Son gives life to whomever he wishes. The Father judges no one but has given all judgment to the Son, so that all may honor the Son just as they honor the Father. Anyone who does not honor the Son does not honor the Father who sent him. Very truly, I tell you, the hour is coming, and is now here, when the dead will hear the voice of the Son of God, and those who hear will live. For just as the Father has life in himself, so he has granted the Son also to have life in himself; and he has given him authority to execute judgment, because he is the Son of Man (John 5, 19-23, 25-27 NRSV).' "

The Bread of Life Discourse in John's Gospel cut to the core of the identity and the authority of Jesus. "Do not work for the food that perishes, but for the food that endures for eternal life, which the Son of Man will give you. For it is on him that God the Father has set his seal. This indeed is the will of my Father, that all who see the Son and believe in him have eternal life, and I will raise them up on the last day (John 6, 27, 40 NRSV)."

Over and over in the Gospel of John, Jesus stresses that he does not act on his own, but on the instructions of his heavenly Father. "So Jesus said … When you lift up the Son of Man, then you will realize that I AM, and that I do nothing on my own, but I say only what the Father taught me. The one who sent me is with me. He has not left me alone, because I always do what is pleasing to him (John 8, 28-29 NRSV)."

Jesus healed the man born blind and the religious leaders threw the man out of the synagogue (John 9, 1-34) "When Jesus heard that they had thrown him out, he found him and said, 'Do you believe in the Son of Man?' He answered and said, 'Who is he, sir, that I may believe in him?' Jesus said to him, 'You have seen him and the one speaking with you is he.' He said, 'I do believe, Lord,' and he worshipped him (John 9, 35-38 NRSV)."

Jesus reigns over life and death. Remember, he raised Lazarus from the dead (John 11). Informed that Lazarus was ill, Jesus proclaimed, 'This illness is not to end in death, but is for the glory of God, that the Son of God may be glorified through it (John 11, 4 NRSV).' "

Jesus knew that he would soon die. " 'The hour has come for the Son of Man to be glorified. Amen, amen, I say to you, unless a grain of wheat falls into. he ground and dies, it remains just a grain of wheat; but if it dies, it produces much fruit (John 12, 23 NRSV).' "

In his Last Supper discourse, Jesus told his disciples, " 'Amen, amen, I say to you, whoever believes in me will do the works that I do, and will do greater ones than these, because I am going to the Father. And whatever you ask in my name, I will do, so that the Father may be glorified in the Son. If you ask anything of me in my name, I will do it (John 14, 12-14 NRSV).' "

Jesus always sought to honor his Father. In his prayer which we often call his high priestly prayer, he prayed, " '... Father, the hour has come. Give glory to your son, so that your son may glorify you ... (John 17, 1b NRSV).'"

After his resurrection, "...Jesus did many other signs in the presence of his disciples, which are not written in this book. But these are written so that you may come to believe that Jesus is the Messiah, the Son of God, and that through believing you may have life in his name (John 20, 30, 31 NRSV)."

"Now when Jesus came into the region of Caesarea Philippi ,he asked his disciples, 'Who do people say that the Son of Man is?' And they said, 'Some say John the Baptist but others Elijah, and still others Jeremiah or one of the prophets.' He said to them, 'But who do you say that I am?' Simon Peter answered, 'You are the Messiah, the son of the living God.' And Jesus answered him, 'Blessed are you, Simon, son of Jonah! For flesh and blood has not revealed this to you, but my Father in heaven. And I tell you, you are Peter, and on this rock I will build my church, and the gates of Hades will not prevail against it. I will you the keys of the kingdom of heaven, and whatever you bind on earth will be bound in heaven, and whatever you loose on earth will be loosed in heaven.' Then he sternly ordered the disciples not to tell anyone that he was the Messiah (Matthew 16, 13-20 NRSV)."

Jesus is very clear in telling his followers that there is a price tag to following him and being his disciple. It is not going to be a bed of roses!

"Then Jesus told his disciples, 'If any want to become my followers ,let them deny themselves and take up their cross and follow me. For those who want to save their life will lose it, and those who lose their life for my sake will find it. For what will it profit them if they gain the whole world but forfeit their life? Or what will they give in return for their life. For the Son of Man is to come with his angels in the glory of his Father, and then he will repay everyone for what he has done. Truly I tell you, there are some standing here who will not taste death before they see the Son of Man coming into his kingdom (Matthew 16, 24-28 NRSV).'"

The passage about the conditions of discipleship is also found in Mark 8, 34-9,1 and in Luke 9, 23-27. Jesus refers to himself as Son of man.

Jesus tells his disciples that he will die at the hands of the religious leaders. This disclosure is preceded by God the Father again revealing Jesus as his Son. The Transfiguration is recounted in the Gospels of Matthew, Mark, and Luke. These leaders are, in fact, religious "executives," those who merely use God-words to feed their own egos and to further their own careers. It happened then and it happens now.

"Six days later, Jesus took with him Peter and James and his brother John and led them up a high mountain, by themselves. And he was transfigured before them, and his face shone like the sun, and his clothes became dazzling white. Suddenly there appeared to them Moses and Elijah talking with him. Then Peter said to Jesus, 'Lord, it is good for us to be here; if you wish, I will make three dwellings here, one for you, one for Moses, and one for Elijah.' While he was still speaking, suddenly a bright cloud overshadowed them, and from the cloud a voice said, 'This is my Son, the Beloved; with him I am well pleased; listen to him!' When the disciples heard this, they fell to the ground and were overcome by fear. But Jesus came and touched them, saying, 'Get up and do not be afraid.' And when they looked up, they saw no one except Jesus himself alone. As they were coming down the mountain, Jesus ordered them, 'Tell no one about the vision until after the Son of Man has been raised from the dead.' And the disciples asked him, 'Why, then, do the scribes say that Elijah must come first?' He replied, 'Elijah is indeed coming and will restore all things; but I tell you that Elijah has already come, and they did not recognize him, but they did to him whatever they pleased. So also the Son of Man is about to suffer at their hands.' Then the disciples understood that he was speaking to them about John the Baptist (Matthew 17, 1-13 NRSV)."

The Transfiguration is also recounted in Mark 9, 2-8 and Luke 9, 28-36. God the Father speaks from the cloud and says that Jesus is his Son.

"And as they were gathering in Galilee, Jesus said to them, 'The Son of man is to be delivered into the hands of men, and they will kill him, and he will be raised on the third day.' And they were greatly distressed (Matthew 17, 22-23)."

The second prediction of the Passion is also told in Mark 9, 30-32 and in Luke 9, 43b-45.

Jesus came specifically to seek out and find those who were "lost." Matthew's Gospel tells how Jesus warned against leading others astray. His disciples were busy wondering who was going to be "great" in the kingdom of Heaven.

"At that time the disciples came to Jesus and asked, 'Who is the greatest in the kingdom of heaven?' He called a child, whom he put among them, and said, 'Truly I tell you, unless you change and become like children, you will never enter the kingdom of heaven. Whoever becomes humble like this child is the greatest in the kingdom of heaven. Whoever welcomes one such child in my name welcomes me (Matthew 18, 1-5 NRSV)."

Jesus, Son of God and Son of man, refers to his Father.

"See that you never despise any of these little one ones, for I tell you that their angels in heaven are continually in the presence of my Father in heaven. For the Son of man has come to save what was lost.'

'Tell me. Suppose a man has a hundred sheep and one of them strays; will he not leave the ninety-nine on the hillside and go in search of the stray? In truth I tell you, if he finds it, it gives him more joy than do the ninety-nine that did not stray at all. Similarly, it is never the will of your Father in heaven that any one of these little ones should be lost (Matthew 18, 10-14).' "

Although the cost of following Jesus is high, the rewards are more than commensurate. Peter, as usual, voiced the silent questions of others.

"… Peter said … , 'Look, we have left everything and followed you. What then will we have?' Jesus said to them, 'Truly I tell you, at the renewal of all things, when the Son of Man is seated on the throne of his glory, you who have followed me will also sit on twelve thrones, judging the twelve tribes of Israel. And everyone who has left houses or brothers or sisters or father or mother or children or fields, for my name's sake, will receive a hundred-fold, and will inherit eternal life. But many who are first now will be last, and the last will be first (Matthew 19, 27-30 NRSV).' "

"When Jesus was going up to Jerusalem, he took the twelve disciples aside by themselves, and said to them on the way, 'See, we are going up to Jerusalem, and the Son of Man will be handed over to the chief priests and scribes, and they will condemn him to death; then they will hand him over to the Gentiles to be mocked and flogged and crucified; and on the third day he will be raised (Matthew 20, 17-19 NRSV).' "

The third prediction of the Passion is also recounted in Mark 10, 32-34 and in Luke 18, 31-34. Jesus refers to himself as Son of Man.

"Then the mother of the sons of Zebedee came to him with her sons, and kneeling before him, she asked a favor of him. And he said to her, 'What do you want?' She said to him, 'Declare that these two sons of mine will sit, one at your right hand and one at your left, in your kingdom.' But Jesus answered, 'You do not know what you are asking. Are you able to drink the cup that I am about to drink?' They said to him, 'We are able.' He said to them, 'You will indeed drink my cup, but to sit at my right hand and at my left, this is not mine to grant, but it is for those for whom it has been prepared by my Father. When the ten heard it, they were angry with the two brothers. But Jesus called them to him and said, 'You know that the rulers of the Gentiles lord it over them, and their great ones are tyrants over them. It shall not be so among you, but whoever wishes to be great among you must be your servant, and whoever wishes to be first among you must be your slave, just as the Son of Man came not to be served but to serve, and to give his life a ransom for many (Matthew 20, 20-28 NRSV).' "

This passage about ambition is also found in Mark 10, 35-45 and in Luke 22, 24-27. In Luke's account, Jesus asks his followers, "For who is greater, the one who is at the table or the one who serves? Is it not the one at the table? But I am among you as one who serves (Luke 22, 27)."

"As they were leaving Jericho, a large crowd followed him. There were two blind men sitting by the roadside. When they heard that Jesus was passing by, they shouted, 'Lord, have mercy on us, Son of David!' The crowd sternly ordered them to be quiet; but they shouted even more loudly, 'Have mercy on us, Lord, Son of David!' Jesus stood still and called them, saying, 'What do you want me to do for you?' They said to him, 'Lord, let our eyes be opened.' Moved with compassion, Jesus touched their eyes. Immediately they regained their sight and followed him (Matthew 20, 29-34 NRSV)."

Jesus is also referred to as Son of David in the parallel accounts in Mark 10, 46-54 and in Luke 18, 35-43.

When Jesus, humbly mounted on a donkey, entered Jerusalem, he was greeted by the crowd shouting,

" 'Hosanna to the Son of David! Blessed is the one who comes in the name of the Lord! Hosanna in the highest heaven!' When he entered Jerusalem, the whole city was in turmoil, asking, 'Who is this?' The crowds were saying, 'This is the prophet Jesus from Nazareth in Galilee (Matthew 21, 9-11 NRSV).' "

"Now while the Pharisees were gathered together, Jesus asked them this question. 'What do you think of the Messiah? Whose son is he?' They said to him, 'The son of David.' He said to them, 'How is it then that David, by the Spirit, calls him Lord, saying, 'The Lord said to my Lord, 'Sit at my right hand, until I put your enemies under your feet'? If David thus calls him Lord how can he be his son?' No one was able to give him an answer, nor from that day did anyone dare to ask him any more questions (Matthew 22, 41-46 NRSV)."

Jesus warns his followers to be very wary of those claiming to be "Messiah" or "Christ." He warns, in the Gospels of Matthew, Mark, and Luke, that before his return, there will be false "Messiahs."

" 'Then if anyone says to you, 'Look! Here is the Messiah! or "There he is!' – do not believe it. For false messiahs and false prophets will appear and produce great signs and omens, to lead astray, if possible, even the elect. Take note, I have told you beforehand.

So, if they say to you, 'Look! He is in the wilderness,' do not go out. If they say, 'Look! He is in the inner rooms,' do not believe it. For as the lightening comes from the east and flashes as far as the west, so will be the coming of the Son of Man.

'Immediately after the suffering of those days, the sun will be darkened, and the moon will not give its light; the stars will fall from heaven, and the powers of heaven will be shaken. Then the sign of the Son of Man will appear in heaven, and all the tribes of the earth will mourn, and they will see 'the Son of Man coming on the clouds of heaven' with power and great glory. And he will send out his angels with a loud trumpet call, and they will gather his elect from the four winds from one end of heaven to the other.

From the fig tree learn its lesson: as soon as its branch becomes tender and puts forth its leaves, you know that summer is near. So also, when you see all these things, you know that he is near, at the very gates. Truly I tell you, this generation will not pass away until all these things have taken place. Heaven and earth will pass away, but my words will not pass away. But about that day and hour no one knows, neither the angels of heaven, nor the Son, but only the Father.

For as the days of Noah were, so will be the coming of the Son of Man. For as in those days before the flood they were eating and drinking, marrying and giving in marriage, until the day Noah entered the ark, and they nothing until the flood came and swept them all away, so too will be the coming of the Son of Man. Then two will be in the field; one will be taken and one will be left. Two women will be grinding meal together; one will be taken and one will be left.

Keep awake therefore, for you do not know on what day your Lord is coming. But understand this: if the owner of the house had known in what part of the night the thief was coming, he would have stayed awake and would not have let his house be broken into. Therefore you also must be ready, for the Son of Man is coming at an unexpected hour (Matthew 24, 23-27, 29-44 NRSV).' "

Read also in Mark 13, 24-27 and in Luke 21, 25-28 about Jesus, the Son of man, coming again in glory! I can hardly wait! How about you?

Jesus, the Son of God and Son of Mary will return as the Bridegroom for his bride, the Church.

" 'Then the kingdom of heaven shall be compared to ten maidens who took their lamps and went to meet the bridegroom. Five of them were foolish, and five were wise. For when the foolish took their lamps, they took no oil with them; but the wise took flasks of oil with their lamps. As the bridegroom was delayed, they all slumbered and slept. But at midnight there was a cry, 'Behold the bridegroom! Come out to meet him.' Then all those maidens rose and trimmed their lamps. And the foolish said to the wise, 'Give us some of your oil, for our lamps are going out.' But the wise replied, 'Perhaps there will not be enough for us and for you; go rather to the dealers and buy for yourselves.' And while they went to buy, the bridegroom came, and those who were ready went in with him to the marriage feast; and the door was shut. Afterward the other maidens came also, saying, 'Lord, Lord, open to us.' But he replied, 'Truly, I say to you, I do not know you.' Watch therefore, for you know neither the day nor the hour (Matthew 25, 1-14)."

"When the Son of man comes in his glory, and all the angels with him, then he will sit on the throne of his glory. All the nations will be gathered before him, and he will separate people one from another as a shepherd separates the sheep from the goats, and he will put the sheep at his right hand and the goats at the left. Then the king will say to those at his right hand, 'Come, you that are blessed by my Father, inherit the kingdom prepared for you from the foundation of the world; for I was hungry and you gave me food, I was thirsty and you gave me something to drink, I was a stranger and you welcomed me, I was naked and you gave me clothing, I was sick and you took care of me, I was in prison and you visited me.' Then the righteous will answer him, 'Lord, when was it that we saw you hungry and gave you food, or thirsty and gave you something to drink? And when was it that we saw you a stranger and welcomed you, or naked and we gave you clothing? And when was it that we saw you sick or in prison and visited you?/ And the king will answer them, 'Truly I tell you, just as you did it to one of the least of these who are members of my family, you did it to me.' Then he will say to those at his left hand, 'You that are accursed, depart from me into the eternal fire prepared for the devil and his angels; for I was hungry and you gave me no food, I was thirsty and you gave me nothing to drink, I was a stranger and you did not welcome me, naked and you did not give me clothing, sick and in prison and you did not visit me.' Then they also will answer, 'Lord, when was it that we saw you hungry or thirsty or a stranger or naked or sick or in prison, and did not take care of you?' And he will answer them, 'Truly I tell you, just as you did not do it to one of the least of these, you did not do it for me.' And these will go away into eternal punishment, but the righteous into eternal life (Matthew 25, 31-46 NRSV)'"

Jesus reminded his disciples that "'... the Passover is coming, and the Son of man will be handed over to be crucified (Matthew 26, 2 NRSV).'"

Referring to his imminent betrayal by Judas, Jesus said, " 'The Son of man goes as it is written of him, but woe to that one by whom the Son of man is betrayed (Matthew 26, 24 NRSV)!'"

The prediction of Judas' tragic betrayal is recounted in Mark 14, 17-25 and in Luke 22, 14-38.

After the Passover meal, Jesus left to pray to his Father. Observing his sleeping disciples, he asked, "Are you still sleeping and taking your rest? Behold, the hour is at hand, and the Son of man is betrayed into the hands of sinners. Rise, let us be going; see, my betrayer is at hand (Matthew 26, 45-46)."

Jesus also refers to himself as Son of man in the parallel passage in Mark 14, 41.

Because of the silence of Jesus before his interrogators, the high priest said to him, " 'I abjure you by the living God, tell us if you are the Christ, the Son of God.' Jesus said to him, 'You have said so. But I tell you, hereafter you will see the Son of man seated at the right hand of Power, and coming on the clouds of heaven (Matthew 26, 63-64).'"

In the parallel passage in Mark, the high priest asked Jesus, " 'Are you the Messiah, the Son of the Blessed One?' Jesus said, 'I am; and 'you will see the Son of Man seated at the right hand of the Power.' and 'coming with the clouds of heaven (Mark 14, 61b-62).'"

At the crucifixion, Jesus was mocked in many cruel ways. In addition to the physical torture, he was subjected to ridicule over his identity.

"And those who passed by derided him, wagging their heads and saying, 'He saved others; he cannot save himself. He is the King of Israel; let him come down now from the cross, and we will believe in him. He trusts in God; let God deliver him now, if he desires him; for he said, 'I am the Son of God (Matthew 27, 39-43).'"

On the cross ... about three o'clock Jesus cried with a loud voice, 'Eli, Eli, lema sabachthani?' that is, 'My God, my God, why have you forsaken me?' Then Jesus cried again with a loud voice and breathed his last. At that moment the curtain of the temple was torn in two, from top to bottom. The earth shook, and the rocks were split. The tombs also were opened, and many bodies of the saints were raised. After his resurrection they came out of the tombs and entered the holy city and appeared to many. Now when the centurion and those with him, who were keeping watch over Jesus, saw the earthquake and what took place, they were terrified and said, 'Truly this man was God's Son (Matthew 27, 46, 50-54 NRSV)!' "

In the Gospel of Mark, we also read that the centurion acknowledged, " 'Truly this man was the Son of God (Mark 15, 39).' "

After the Resurrection and after spending time with his followers, Jesus, Son of God and Son of Man, prepared to return to his Father. "Now the eleven disciples went to Galilee, to the mountain to which Jesus had directed them. And when they saw him they worshiped him; but some doubted. And Jesus same and said to them, 'All authority in heaven and on earth has been given to me. Go therefore and make disciples of all nations, baptizing them in the name of the Father and of the Son and of the Holy Spirit, teaching them to observe all that I have commanded you; and lo, I am with you always, to the end of the age
(Matthew 28, 16-20).' "

Before Stephen was martyred by the furious religious leaders, he first recounted the history of Israel, rebuked the leaders for their murder of the prophets and of Jesus himself. "Now when they heard these things they were enraged, and they ground their teeth against him. But he, full of the Holy Spirit, gazed into heaven and saw the glory of God, and Jesus standing at the right hand of God; and he said, 'Behold, I see the heavens opened, and the Son of man standing at the right hand of God
(Acts 7, 54-56).' "

Saul stood by and consented with those who killed Stephen. After his dramatic conversion on the road to Damascus, he went to the

synagogues and "proclaimed Jesus saying, 'He is the Son of God
(Acts 9, 20).' "

If God can change the heart of one so filled with misguided zeal as the one we now call St. Paul, then God can change the heart of anyone. This should give us courage never to give up loving and praying for others.

Paul then went on to preach in many places. In Antioch, he said, "And we bring you the good news that what God promised to our ancestors he has fulfilled for us, their children, by raising Jesus; as also it is written in the second psalm,

> 'You are my Son,
> today I have begotten you (Acts 13, 32-33 NRSV).' "

Paul's letter to the Romans begins, "Paul, a servant of Jesus Christ, called to be an apostle, set apart for the gospel of God which he promised beforehand through his prophets in the holy scriptures, the gospel concerning his Son, who was descended from David according to the flesh and designated Son of God in power according to the Spirit of holiness by his resurrection from the dead, Jesus Christ our Lord ... (Romans 1, 1-4)."

"For if while we were enemies we were reconciled to God by the death of his Son, much more, now that we are reconciled, shall we be saved by his life (Romans 5, 10)."

"Thus, condemnation will never come to those who are in Christ Jesus, because the law of the Spirit which gives life in Christ Jesus has set you free from the law of sin and death. What the Law could not do because of the weakness of human nature, God did, by sending his own Son in the same human nature as any sinner to be a sacrifice for sin, and condemning sin in that human nature. This was so that the Law's requirements might be fully satisfied in us as we direct our lives not by our natural inclinations but by the spirit (Acts 8, 1-4)."

"We know that in everything God works for good with those who love him, who are called according to his purpose. For those whom he foreknew he also predestined to be conformed to the image of his Son, in order that he might be the first-born among many brethren. And those whom he called he also justified; and those whom he justified he also glorified. What then shall we say to this? If God is for us, who is against us? He who did not spare his own Son but gave him up for us all, will he not also give us all things with him? Who shall bring any charge against God's elect? It is God who justifies; who is to condemn? It is Christ Jesus, who died, yes, who was raised from the dead, who is at the right hand of God, who indeed intercedes for us? Who shall separate us from the love of Christ? Shall tribulation, or distress, or persecution, or famine, or nakedness, or peril, or sword? As it is written,

> 'For thy sake we are being killed all
> the day long
> we are regarded as sheep to be

slaughtered.'

No, in all these things we are more than conquerors through him who loved us. For I am sure that neither death, nor life, nor angels, nor principalities, nor things present, nor things to come, nor powers, nor height, nor depth, nor anything else in all creation, will be able to separate us from the love of God in Christ Jesus our Lord (Romans 8, 28-39)."

"I give thanks to God always for you because of the grace of God which was given you in Christ Jesus, that in every way you were enriched in him with all speech and all knowledge -- even as the testimony to Christ was confirmed among you -- so that you are not lacking in any spiritual gift, as you wait for the revealing of our Lord Jesus Christ; who will sustain you to the end, guiltless in the day of our Lord Jesus Christ. God is faithful, by whom you were called into the fellowship of his Son, Jesus Christ our Lord (1 Corinthians 1, 4-9)."

"For the Son of God, Jesus Christ, whom we preached among you ... was not Yes and No; but in him it is always Yes. For all the promises of God find their Yes in him (2 Corinthians 1, 19-20a)."

"But when he who had set me apart before I was born, and had called me through his grace, was pleased to reveal his Son to me, in order that I might preach him among the Gentiles, I did not confer with flesh and blood, nor did I go up to Jerusalem to those who were apostles before me, but I went away into Arabia; and again I returned to Damascus (Galatians 1, 15-17)."

Paul needed time alone to become more deeply acquainted on a personal level with Jesus, the Son of God. Paul had an intellectual grasp of the power and majesty of God the Father. However, meeting this "God in the flesh," this incarnate God, this mysterious Jesus, was something far beyond the power of Paul's intellect. Jesus was calling Paul, as he is calling you and me, to spend time to get to know him. This will involve time in solitude, time in prayer, and time reading the Scriptures. It is also very necessary to be in community with other Christians, but this cannot substitute for our own personal time alone with Jesus.

"I have been crucified with Christ; it is no longer I who live, but Christ who lives in me; and the life I now live in the flesh I live by faith in the Son of God, who loved me and gave himself for me (Galatians 2, 20)."

"But when the fullness of time had come, God sent his Son, born of a woman, born under the law, in order to redeem those who were under the law, so that we might receive adoption as children. And because you are children, God has sent the Spirit of his Son into our hearts, crying, 'Abba! Father!' So you are no longer a slave but a child, and if a child then also an heir, through God (Galatians 4, 4-7 NRSV)."

"The gifts he gave were that some would be apostles, some prophets, some evangelists, some pastors and teachers, to equip the saints for the work of ministry, for building up the body of Christ, until all of us come to the unity of the faith and of the knowledge of the Son of God, to maturity, to the measure of the full stature of Christ. We must no longer be children, tossed to and fro and blown about by every wind of doctrine, by people's trickery, by their craftiness in deceitful scheming. But speaking the truth in love, we must grow up into him who is the head, into Christ, from whom the whole body, joined and knit together by every ligament with which it is equipped, as each part is working properly, promotes the body's growth in building itself up in love (Ephesians 4, 11-16)."

"May you be strengthened with all power, according to his glorious might, for all endurance and patience with joy, giving thanks to the Father, who has qualified us to share in the inheritance of the saints in light. He has delivered us from the dominion of darkness and transferred us to the kingdom of his beloved Son, in whom we have redemption, the forgiveness of sins (Colossians 1, 11-14)."

Paul wrote to the Thessalonians reminding them how they had "turned to God from idols, to serve a living and true God, and to wait for his Son from heaven …(1 Thessalonians 1, 9-10a)."

"Long ago God spoke to our ancestors in many and various ways by the prophets, but in these last days he has spoken to us by a Son, whom he appointed heir of all things, through whom he also created the worlds. He is the reflection of God's glory and the exact imprint of God's very being, and he sustains all things by his powerful word. When he had made purification for sins, he sat down at the right hand of the Majesty on high, having become as much superior to angels as the name he has inherited is more excellent than theirs (Hebrews 11, 1-4 NRSV)."

The writer to the Hebrews is very careful to differentiate between Jesus and the angels.

"For to which of the angels did God ever say, 'You are my Son; today I have begotten you'? Or again, 'I will be his Father, and he will be my Son'? And again, when he brings the firstborn into the world, he says, 'Let all the angels worship him.' Of the angels he says, 'He makes his angels winds, and his servants flames of fire.' But of the Son he says,

'Your throne, O God, is forever and ever, and the righteous scepter is the scepter of your kingdom. You have loved righteousness and hated wickedness; therefore God, your God, has anointed you with the oil of gladness beyond your companions (Hebrews 1, 5-9 NRSV).' "

"Now Moses was faithful in all God's house as a servant, to testify to the things that would be spoken later. Christ, however, was faithful over God's house as a son, and we are his house if we hold firm the confidence and the pride that belongs to hope (Hebrews 3, 5, 6 NRSV)."

"Since then have a great high priest who has passed through the heavens, Jesus, the Son of God, let us hold fast our confession. For we have not a high priest who is unable to sympathize with our weaknesses, but one who in every respect has been tempted as we are, yet without sin. Let us then with confidence draw near to the throne of grace, that we may receive mercy and find grace to help in time of need (Hebrews 4, 14-16)."

"Every high priest chosen from among mortals is put in charge of things pertaining to God on their behalf, to offer gifts and sacrifices for sins. He is able to deal gently with the ignorant and wayward, since he himself is subject to weakness; and because of this he must offer sacrifice for his own sins as well as for those of the people. And one does not presume to take this honor, but takes it only when called by God, just as Aaron was. So also Christ did not glorify himself in becoming a high priest, but was appointed by the one who said to him, 'You are my Son, today I have begotten you'; as he says also in another place, 'You are a priest forever, according to the order of Melchizedek.' In the days of his flesh, Jesus offered up prayers and supplications, with loud cries and tears, to the one who was able to save him from death, and he was heard because of his reverent submission. Although he was a Son, he learned obedience through what he suffered; and having been made perfect, he became the source of eternal salvation for all who obey him, having been designated by God a high priest ... (Hebrews 5, 1-10 NRSV).' "

"Anyone who has violated the law of Moses dies without mercy 'on the testimony of two or three witnesses.' How much worse punishment do you think will be deserved by those who have spurned the Son of God, profaned the blood of the covenant by which they were sanctified, and outraged the Spirit of grace? For we know the one who said, 'Vengeance is mine, I will repay.' And again, 'It is a fearful thing to fall into the hands of the living God (Hebrews 10, 28-31 NRSV).' "

"For we did not follow cleverly devised myths when we made known to you the power and coming of our Lord Jesus Christ, but we were eyewitnesses of his majesty. For when he received honor and glory from God the Father and the voice was borne to him by the Majestic Glory, 'This is my beloved Son, with whom I am well pleased,' we heard this voice borne from heaven, for we were with him on the holy mountain (2 Peter 1, 16-18)."

"That which was from the beginning, which we have heard, which we have seen with our eyes, which we have looked upon and touched with our hands, concerning the word of life -- the life was made manifest, and we saw it, and testify to it, and proclaim to you the eternal life which was with the Father and was manifest to us -- that which we have seen and heard we proclaim also to you, so that you may have fellowship with us; and our fellowship is with the Father and with his Son Jesus Christ (1 John 1, 1-3)."

"This is the message we have heard from him and proclaim to you, that God is light and in him is no darkness at all. If we say we have fellowship with him while we walk in darkness, we lie and do not live according to the truth; but if we walk in the light, as he is in the light, we have fellowship with one another, and the blood of Jesus his Son cleanses us from all sin (1 John 1, 5-7)."

"Who is the liar if not one who claims that Jesus is not the Christ? This is the Antichrist, who denies both the Father and the Son. Whoever denies the Son cannot have the Father either; whoever acknowledges the Son has the Father too. Let what you heard in the beginning remain in you; as long as what you heard in the beginning remains in you, you will remain in the Son and in the Father (1 John 2, 22-24)."

"The reason the Son of God appeared was to destroy the works of the devil (1 John 3, 8)."

"By this we shall know that we are of the truth, and reassure our hearts before him whenever our hearts condemn us; for God is greater than our hearts, and he knows everything. Beloved, if our hearts do not condemn us, we have confidence before God; and we receive from him whatever we ask, because we keep his commandments and do what pleases him. And this is his commandment, that we should believe in the name of his Son Jesus Christ and love one another, just as he commanded us (1 John 3, 19-23)."

"In this the love of God was made manifest among us, that God sent his only Son into the world, so that we might live through him. In this is love, not that we loved God but that he loved us and sent his Son to be the expiation for our sins. Beloved, if God so loved us, we also ought to love one another (1 John 4, 7-11)."

"God abides in those who confess that Jesus is the Son of God, and they abide in God (1 John 4, 15 NRSV)."

"Who is it that conquers the world but the one who believes that Jesus is the Son of God (1 John 5, 5 NRSV)?"

"Those who believe in the Son of God have the testimony in their hearts. Those who do not believe in God have made him a liar by not believing in the testimony that God has given concerning his Son. And this is the testimony: God gave us eternal life. and this life is in his Son. Whoever has the Son has life; whoever does not have the Son does not have life. I write these things to you who believe in the name of the Son of God, so that you may know that you have eternal life (1 John 5, 10-13 NRSV)."

"And we know that the Son of God has come and given us understanding, to know him who is true; and we are in him who is true, in his Son Jesus Christ. This is the true God and eternal life (1 John 5, 20)."

"Grace, mercy, and peace will be with us from God the Father and from Jesus Christ, the Father's Son, in truth and love. Everyone who does not abide in the teaching of Christ, but goes beyond it, does not have God; whoever abides in the teaching has both the Father and the Son (2 John 3, 9 NRSV)."

The last book of the Bible, the Revelation to John, tells of the appearance of Jesus, the risen and glorified Son of God.

"I, John, your brother who share with you in Jesus the persecution and the kingdom and the patient endurance, was on the island called Patmos because of the word of God and the testimony of Jesus. I was in the spirit on the Lord's day, and I heard behind me a loud voice like a trumpet saying, 'Write in a book what you see and send it to the seven churches, to Ephesus, to Smyrna, to Pergamum, to Thyatira, to Sardis, to Philadelphia, and to Laodicia. Then I turned to see whose voice it was that spoke to me, and on turning I saw seven golden lampstands, and in the midst of the lampstands I saw one like the Son of Man, clothed with a long robe and with a golden sash across his chest. His head and his hair were white as white wool, white as snow; his eyes were like a flame of fire, and his feet were like burnished bronze, refined as in a furnace, and his voice was like the sound of many waters. In his right hand he held seven stars, and from his mouth came a sharp, two-edged sword, and his face was like the sun shining in full force. When I saw him, I fell at his feet as though dead. But he placed his right hand on me, saying, 'Do not be afraid; I am the first and the last, and the living one. I was dead, and see, I am alive forever and ever; and I have the keys of Death and of Hades. Now write what you have seen, what is, and what is to take place after this. As for the mystery of the seven stars that you saw in my right hand, and the seven golden lampstands: the seven stars are the angels of the seven churches, and the seven lampstands are the seven churches (Revelation 1, 9-20 NRSV).' "

" 'And to the angel of the church of the church in Thyatira write: These are the words of the Son of God, who has eyes like a flame of fire, and whose feet are like burnished bronze: I know your works – your love, faith, service, and patient endurance. But I have this against you: you tolerate that woman Jezebel, who calls herself a prophet and is teaching and beguiling my servants ... (Revelation 2, 18 – 20a NRSV).' "

As we end this section of reading a number of verses in which Jesus is referred to both as Son of God and Son of Man, it is comforting to note that the One who is so radiantly triumphant and powerful as to hold the keys of death, is also the One who knows all about us.

The above verse mentions specifically that Jesus knows "your love, faith, service, and patient endurance (v. 19)." Sometimes we feel so alone, but we have to remember that Jesus is with us and knows every detail of our lives. Then, we can trust and know that He will work it all out in the best way.

SPIRIT (see Holy Spirit)

STONE (ROCK)

As the patriarch Jacob was dying, he called his sons to be with him and to receive his blessings.

"Joseph is a fruitful bough, a fruitful bough by a spring;
his branches run over the wall.
The archers fiercely attacked him;
they shot at him and pressed him hard.
Yet his bow remained taut, and his arms were made agile
by the hands of the Mighty One of Jacob,
by the name of the Shepherd, the Rock of Israel,
by the God of your father, who will help you,
by the Almighty who will bless you ...
     (Genesis 49, 22-25a NRSV)."

"For the LORD spoke thus to me with his strong hand upon me, and warned me not to walk in the way of this people, saying: 'Do not call conspiracy all that this people call conspiracy, and do not fear what they fear, nor be in dread. But the LORD of hosts, him you shall regard as holy; let him be your fear, and let him be your dread. And he will become a sanctuary, and a stone of offense, and a rock of stumbling to both houses of Israel, a trap and a snare to the inhabitants of Jerusalem. And many shall stumble thereon; they shall be snared and taken (Isaiah 8, 11-15)."

" '… thus says the Lord GOD, See, I am laying in Zion a foundation stone, a tested stone, a precious cornerstone, a sure foundation … (Isaiah 28, 16 NRSV).' "

"Jesus said to them, 'Have you never read in the scriptures: The stone that the builders rejected has become the cornerstone; this was the Lord's doing, and it is amazing in our eyes (Matthew 21, 42 NRSV)?' " The Gospels of Mark (12, 10) and Luke (20, 17-18) also record this passage.

After the healing of the lame man, Peter told the Jewish leaders, "if we are questioned today because of a good deed done to someone who was sick and are asked how this man has been healed, let it be known to all of you, and to all the people of Israel, that this man is standing before you in good health by the name of Jesus Christ of Nazareth, who you crucified, whom God raised from the dead. This Jesus is 'the stone rejected by you, the builders; yet it has become the cornerstone.' There is salvation in no one else, for there is no other name under heaven given among mortals by which we must be saved (Acts 4, 9-12 NRSV).' "

To the faithful believers in Ephesus, Paul writes, "So then you are no longer strangers and sojourners, but you are fellow citizens with the saints and members of the household of God, built upon the foundation of the apostles and prophets, Christ Jesus himself being the cornerstone, in whom the whole structure is joined together and grows into a holy temple in the Lord, in whom you are also built into it for a dwelling place of God in the Spirit (Ephesians 2, 20-22)."

"Come to him [Jesus], a living stone, though rejected by mortals yet chosen and precious in God's sight, and like living stones, let yourselves be built into a spiritual house, to be a holy priesthood, to offer spiritual sacrifices acceptable to God through Jesus Christ. For it stands in scripture: 'See, I am laying in Zion a stone, a cornerstone chosen and precious; and whoever believes in him will not be put to shame.' To you then who believe, he is precious; but for those who do not believe, 'The stone that the builders rejected has become the very head of the corner,' and 'A stone that makes them stumble, and a rock that makes them fall.' They stumble because they disobey the word, as they were destined to do. But you are a chosen race, a royal priesthood, a holy nation, God's own people, in order that you may proclaim the mighty acts of him who called you out of darkness into his marvelous light. Once you were not a people, but now you are God's people; once you had not received mercy, but now you have received mercy (1 Peter 2, 4-10 NRSV).' "

STRENGTH

Throughout Scripture God is portrayed as the giver of strength. Perhaps one of the best-known passages is Isaiah 40,

"... they who wait for the LORD
    shall renew their strength,
they shall mount up with wings
    like eagles,
they shall run and not be weary,
they shall walk and not faint (Isaiah 40, 31)."

There are, however, references in which God is personified as "Strength."

"O my Strength, I will sing praises to thee;
    for thou, O God, art my fortress (Psalm 59, 9)."

"O my Strength, I will sing praises to thee,
    for thou, O God, art my fortress,
the God who shows me steadfast love (Psalm 59, 17)."

SUN

We have seen earlier references to God as "Light." There are other verses referring specifically to God as "sun."

"For the LORD God is a sun and shield,
  he bestows favor and honor.
No good thing does the LORD withhold
  from those who walk uprightly (Psalm 84, 11)."

" 'See, the day is coming, burning like an oven, when all the arrogant and all evildoers will be stubble; the day that comes shall burn them up, says the LORD of hosts, so that it will leave them neither root nor branch. But for you who revere my name the sun of righteousness shall rise, with healing in its wings. You shall go out leaping like calves from the stall. And you shall tread down the wicked, for they will be ashes under the soles of your feet, on the day when I act, says the LORD of hosts (Malachi 4, 1-3 NRSV).' " (This is Malachi 3, 19-21 in some other translations).

The Book of the Revelation tells us that God will be our ultimate light.

"Then the angel showed me the river of life, rising from the throne of God and of the Lamb and flowing crystal-clear. Down in the middle of the city street, on either bank of the river were the trees of life, which bear twelve crops of fruit in a year, one in each month, and the leaves of which are the cure for the nations. The curse of destruction will be abolished. The throne of God and of the Lamb will be in the city; his servants will worship him, they will see him face to face, and his name will be written on their foreheads. And night will be abolished; they will not need lamp light or sunlight, because the Lord God will be shining on them. They will reign for ever and ever (Revelation 22, 1-5)."

TEACHER (See "RABBI")

JUST (UPRIGHT) ONE

"The way of the righteous is level; O Just One, you make smooth the path of the righteous (Isaiah 26, 7 NRSV)."

VINE

The image of Jesus as the true vine is especially easy to grasp for those who live near vineyards. Here in California, I love to see the strong vines spread out over the hillsides. The branches simply draw their life and their strength from the vine and then produce the most beautiful grapes.

Jesus tells us, " 'I am the true vine, and my Father is the vine grower. He removes every branch in me that bears no fruit. Every branch that bears fruit he prunes to make it bear more fruit. You have already been cleansed by the word that I have spoken to you. Abide in me as I abide in you. Just as the branch cannot bear fruit by itself unless it abides in the vine, neither can you unless you abide in me. I am the vine, you are the branches. Those who abide in me and I in them bear much fruit, because apart from me you can do nothing. Whoever does not abide in me is thrown away like a branch and withers; such branches are gathered, thrown into the fire, and burned. If you abide in me, and my words abide in you, ask for whatever you wish, and it will be done for you. My Father is glorified by this, that you bear much fruit and become my disciples (John 15, 1-8 NRSV).' "

(WATER)

The term "water," is not, of course an actual name. It is, however, a way of referring to the life-giving aspect of the Holy Spirit.

"On the last day of the festival, the great day, while Jesus was standing there, he cried out, 'Let anyone who is thirsty come to me, and let the one who believes in me drink. As the scripture has said, 'Out of the believer's heart shall flow rivers of living water.' Now he said this about the Spirit which believers in him were to receive … (John 7, 37-39a NRSV).' "

There had been hints earlier in John's Gospel of this "living water." When Jesus talked with the woman at the well, he told her "… If you knew the gift of God, and who it is that is saying to you, 'Give me a drink,' you would have asked him, and he would have given you living water.' The woman said to him, 'Sir, you have no bucket, and the well is deep. Where do you get that living water? Are you greater than our ancestor Jacob, who gave us the well, and with his sons and flocks drank from it?' Jesus said to her, "Everyone who drinks of this water will be thirsty again, but those who drink of the water that I will give them will never be thirsty. The water that I will give will become in them a spring of water gushing up to eternal life (John 4, 10-14 NRSV).' "

WAY

The puzzled disciple Thomas said to Jesus, "…'Lord, we do not know where you are going. How can we know the way? Jesus said to him, 'I am the way, and the truth, and the life. No one comes to the Father except through me. If you know me, you will know my Father also. From now on you do know him and have seen him (John 14, 5-7 NRSV).' "

The Greek word, "hodos," which we translate as "way." refers to a road, a journey, progress, a route, a mode or means, or a highway.

Numerous times in the Acts of the Apostles, Jesus is referred to as the Way. "The Way" also refers to the Church. Recall the dramatic conversion of Saul, who would become St. Paul.

"Meanwhile Saul, still breathing threats and murder against the disciples of the Lord, went to the high priest and asked him for letters to the synagogues at Damascus, so that if he found any who belonged to the Way, men or women, he might bring them bound to Jerusalem (Acts 9, 1-2 NRSV)."

Paul, in Ephesus, "... entered the synagogue and for three months spoke out boldly, and argued persuasively about the kingdom of God. When some stubbornly refused to believe and spoke evil of the Way before the congregation, he left them, taking the disciples with him .... This continued for two years so that all the residents of Asia, both Jews and Greeks, heard the word of the Lord (Acts 19, 8-10 NRSV)."

There followed a time of extraordinary ministry and miracles. 'Now after these things had been accomplished, Paul resolved in the Spirit to go through Macedonia and Achaia, and then go to Jerusalem. He said, 'After I have gone there, I must also see Rome.' So he sent two of his helpers, Timothy and Erastus, to Macedonia, while he himself stayed for some time longer in Asia. About that time, no little disturbance broke out concerning the Way. (Acts 19, 21-23 NRSV)."

This had to do with the silversmith Demetrius. He was greatly distressed because his business making silver shrines of Diana was being threatened by the preaching of Paul.

Paul, on several occasions, described how he came to know Jesus in a personal way. When he spoke to the Jews in Jerusalem, he said, " 'Brothers and sisters, listen to the defense that I now make before you.' When they heard him addressing them in Hebrew, they became even more quiet. Then he said, 'I am a Jew, born in Tarsus in Cilicia, but brought up in this city at the feet of Gamaliel, educated strictly according to our ancestral law, being zealous for God, just as all of you are today. I persecuted this Way up to the point of death by binding both men and women and putting them in prison ... (Acts 22, 1-4 NRSV).' "

The passage to follow was part of Paul's statement of defense before Felix, the Roman governor of Judea.

" 'But this I admit to you, that according to the Way, which they call a sect, I worship the God of our ancestors, believing everything laid down according to the law or written in the prophets. I have a hope in God – a hope that they themselves also accept – that there will be a resurrection of both the righteous and the unrighteous. Therefore I do my best always to have a clear conscience toward God and all people (Acts 24, 14-16 NRSV).' "

There is a very sad passage to follow, about Felix, the Roman governor of Judea. "At this, Felix, who was fairly well informed about the Way, adjourned the case, saying, 'When Lysias the tribune comes down I will give judgment about your case.' He then gave orders to the centurion that he should be kept under arrest but free from restriction, and that none of his own people should be prevented from seeing to his needs.

Some days later Felix came with his wife Drusilla who was a Jewess. He sent for Paul and gave him a hearing on the subject of faith in Christ Jesus. But when he began to entreat of uprightness, self-control and the coming Judgment, Felix took fright and said, 'You may go for the present; I will send for you when I find it convenient.' At the same time he had hopes of receiving money from Paul, and for this reason he sent for him frequently and had talks with him.

When two years came to an end, Felix was succeeded by Porcius Festus and being anxious to gain favour with the Jews, Felix left Paul in custody (Acts 24, 22-27)."

This is sad because God gave Felix a "window of opportunity." Felix was unable, because of fear and because of his need to play politics, to respond to Christ through the ministry of Paul.

WORD

Many people think of the "Word" as the written word, the book called the Bible. The Bible, itself, however, refers to the Word as a Person, the Lord Jesus Christ.

"In the beginning was the Word and the Word was with God, and the Word was God. He was in the beginning with God; all things were made through him, and without him was not anything made that was made. In him was life, and the life was the light of men. The light shines in the darkness, and the darkness has not overcome it.

There was a man sent from God, whose name was John. He came for testimony, to bear witness to the light, that all might believe through him. He was not the light, but came to bear witness to the light.

The true light that enlightens every man was coming into the world. He was in the world, and the world was made through him, yet the world knew him not. He came to his own home, and his own people received him not. But to all who received him, who believed in his name, he gave power to become children of God; who were born, not of blood nor of the will of the flesh nor of the will of man, but of God.

And the Word became flesh and dwelt among us, full of grace and truth; we have beheld his glory, glory as of the only Son from the

Father. (John bore witness to him, and cried, 'This was he of whom I said, 'He who comes after me ranks before me, for he was before me.') And from his fulness have we all received, grace upon grace. For the law was given through Moses; grace and truth came through Jesus Christ. No one has ever seen God; the only Son, who is in the bosom of the Father, he has made him known (John 1, 1-18)."

The writer to the Hebrews summed it up by saying,

"Long ago God spoke to our ancestors in many and various ways by the prophets, but in these last days he has spoken to us by a Son, whom he appointed heir of all things, through whom he also created the worlds. He is the reflection of God's glory and the exact imprint of God's very being, and he sustains all things by his powerful word (Hebrews 1, 1-3a NRSV)."

"We declare to you what was from the beginning, what we have heard, what we have seen with our eyes, what we have looked at and touched with our hands, concerning the word of life – this life was revealed, and we have seen it and testify to it, and declare to you the eternal life that was with the Father and was revealed to us – we declare to you what we have seen and heard so that you also may have fellowship with us; and truly our fellowship is with the Father and with his Son Jesus Christ. We are writing these things so that our joy may be complete (1 John 1, 1-4 NRSV)."

"Then I saw heaven opened, and there was a white horse! Its rider is called Faithful and True, and in righteousness he judges and makes war. His eyes are like a flame of fire, and on his head are many diadems; and he has a name inscribed that no one knows except himself. He is clothed in a robe dipped in blood, and his name is called The Word of God (Revelation 19, 11-13 NRSV)."

Several decades ago, I started this study of the names of God. What I want you, dear reader, to understand is that King Jesus, who came as the suffering servant to live and die for us, will return as KING, the triumphant Lord of all.

I pray for you to know the tender love and forgiveness as well as the mighty power of your coming King. He is present with you now. Simply speak to him, tell him that you need him, ask him to cleanse away your offences and to fill you with the Holy Spirit.

With you, I look forward to the fulfillment of the prophecy in Isaiah:

"On this mountain, the LORD of hosts will make for all peoples a feast of rich food, a feast of well-aged wines, of rich food filled with marrow, of well-aged wines strained clear. And he will destroy on this mountain the shroud that is cast over all peoples, the sheet that is spread over all nations; he will swallow up death forever. Then the Lord GOD will wipe away the tears from all faces, and the disgrace of his people he will take away from the earth, for the LORD has spoken. It will be said on that day, 'Lo, this is our God; we have waited for him, so that he might save us. This is the LORD for whom we have waited; let us be glad and rejoice in his salvation (Isaiah 25, 6-9 NRSV).'"

A.M.D.G.

Janis Walker is the author of ALLELUIA! A GOSPEL DIARY and other books. She received a Master's of Theology degree from St. Patrick's Seminary and also studied at Fuller Theological Seminary and the Graduate Theological Union in Berkeley. She was received into the Roman Catholic Church on May 13, 1998, in a Chrism Mass for Christian Unity in Rossi Chapel at the Jesuit Retreat Center. Janis lives with her family in California and continues her interest in the ecclesial effects of the Oxford Movement and the legacy of Cardinal Newman.

A.M.D.G.

You may order additional copies of this book

from www.amazon.com, www.barnesandnoble.com,

or through your favorite bookstore.

www.ingramcontent.com/pod-product-compliance
Lightning Source LLC
Chambersburg PA
CBHW051756040426
42446CB00007B/388